AF836051

Authors

Jeanette Jolley and John Powrie

SHELL EDUCATION

Credits

Associate Editor
Josh Roby

Assistant Editor
Leslie Huber, M.A.

Editorial Director
Dona Herweck Rice

Editor-in-Chief
Sharon Coan, M.S.Ed.

Editorial Manager
Gisela Lee, M.A.

Creative Director
Lee Aucoin

Illustration Manager
Timothy J. Bradley

Print Production Manager
Don Tran

Interior Layout Design
Robin Erickson

Publisher
Corinne Burton, M.A.Ed.

Shell Education
5301 Oceanus Drive
Huntington Beach, CA 92649-1030
http://www.shelleducation.com
ISBN 978-1-4258-0167-0

© *2008 Shell Educational Publishing, Inc.*

Reprinted 2010

The classroom teacher may reproduce copies of materials in this book for classroom use only. The reproduction of any part for an entire school or school system is strictly prohibited. No part of this publication may be transmitted, stored, or recorded in any form without written permission from the publisher.

Table of Contents

Table of Contents (cont.)

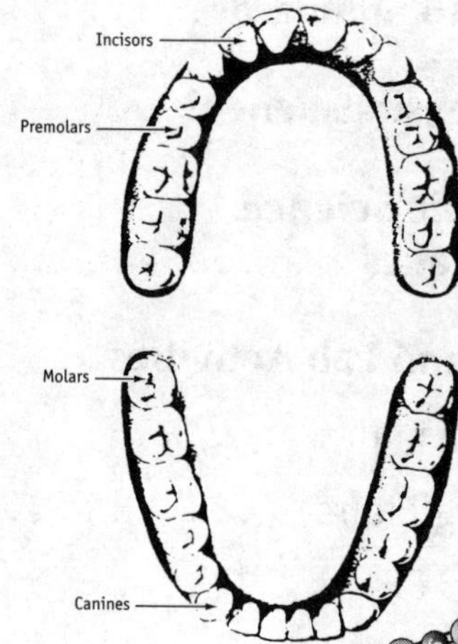

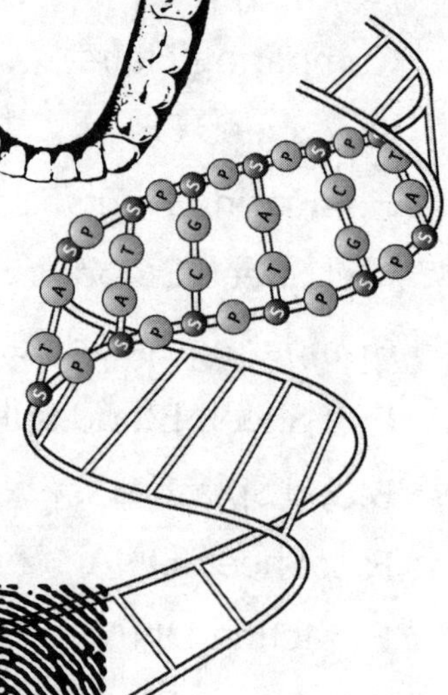

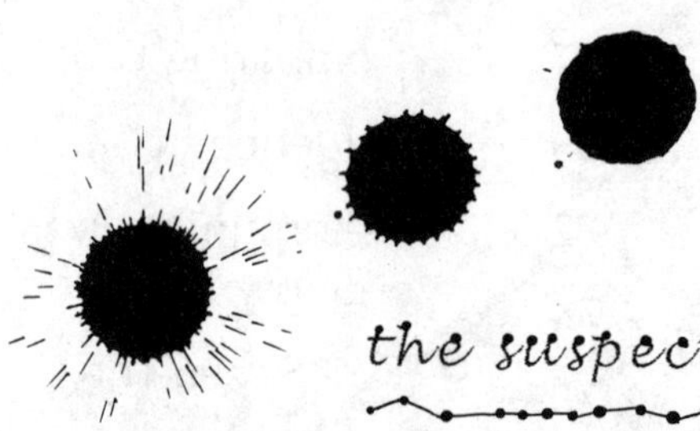

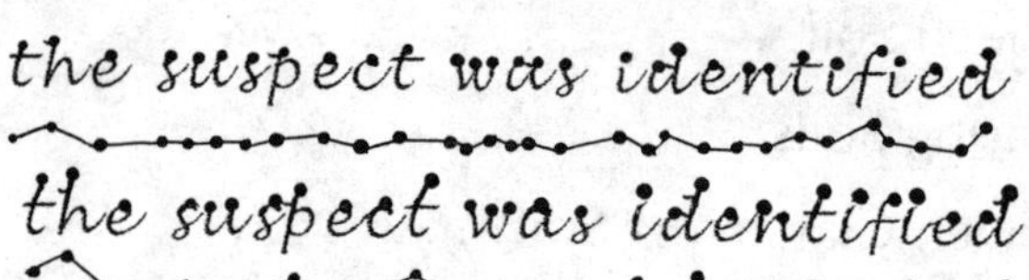

Introduction and Research Base

Inquiry-Based Learning

Over three decades ago, the American Association for the Advancement of Science (AAAS) began a three-phase project to develop and promote science literacy: Project 2061. The project was established with the understanding that just doing more science is not the answer (1989, p. 4).

As Project 2061 began, researchers questioned the appropriateness and effectiveness of science textbooks and methods of instruction. Since textbook instruction puts more emphasis on learning correct answers and less on exploration, collaboration, and inquiry, the AAAS asserts that this manner of instruction actually "impedes progress toward scientific literacy" (1989, p. 14).

This same concern resurfaced over a decade later by Daniels and Zemelman (2004) who call textbooks "unfriendly." When most adults are choosing literature, they do not pick up their child's science textbook. Daniels and Zemelman assert that today's textbooks are best used as references when students need large amounts of information on a particular topic. Instead, they recommend the use of "authentic" sources.

Project 2061 recommends pedagogical practices where the learning of science is as much about the process as the result or outcome (1989, p. 147). Following the nature of scientific inquiry, students ask questions and are actively engaged in the learning process. They collect data and are encouraged to work within teams to investigate the unknown. This method of process learning refocuses the students' learning from knowledge and comprehension to application and analysis. Students may also formulate opinions (synthesis and evaluation) and determine whether their processes were effective or needed revision (evaluation).

The National Science Education Standards view inquiry as "central to science learning" (p. 2 of Overview). In this way, students may develop their understanding of science concepts by combining knowledge with reasoning and thinking skills. Kreuger and Sutton (2001) also report an increase in students' comprehension of text when knowledge learning is coupled with hands-on science activities (p. 52).

Values and Skills

Scientists work under a distinctive set of values. Therefore, according to the AAAS, science education should do the same (1989, p. 133). Students whose learning includes data, a testable hypothesis, and predictability in science will share in the values of the scientists they study. Additionally, "science education is in a particularly strong position to foster three [human] attitudes and values: curiosity, openness to new ideas, and skepticism" (1989, p. 134). *Forensic Science* addresses each of these recommendations by engaging students in thought-provoking, open-ended discussions and projects.

Within the recommendations of skills needed for scientific literacy, the AAAS suggests attention to computation, manipulation and observation, communication, and critical response. These skills are best learned through the process of learning, rather than in the knowledge itself (1989, p. 135).

How to Use This Book

Forensics is a fascinating subject that employs all areas and types of science. To that end, it offers both an excellent platform for science instruction and practice as well as a wide-ranging field for assessment. Because the field is so wide and varied, this book can be utilized in total or in part.

The ideal place to begin is with the introductory overview on forensics and contact traces (pages 11-29). The more students understand about the history and development of forensics, the more they are likely to enjoy the science itself. It may even be worthwhile to supplement this study with readings from some of the classic literary criminalists, such as Sir Arthur Conan Doyle's stories of Sherlock Holmes or Edgar Allan Poe's *The Murders in the Rue Morgue*. You also might read real case studies, easily found on the Internet and in newspaper archives. The real-world, practical applications of science in this realm are almost always intriguing to students and whet their appetites to learn and know more.

Once forensic science as a whole has been introduced, look to the fact sheets and labs that follow for hands-on forensic experiences. The fact sheets provide the necessary overview of the material involved in the lab. The labs allow students to put into practice what they have learned. While the labs may certainly be done without using the fact sheets, to ensure the most successful results, the labs work best when preceded with a study of the fact sheets and provided comprehension questions.

A Note About Safety

It should go without saying, but whenever working with the "stuff" of science, one should always exercise the extremes of caution and safety standards. Because these labs deal with forensics, they sometimes call for organic substances to be used. Such items should only be handled with the strictest safety measures and adherence to school codes. It is likewise true for chemicals and equipment. Be sure that both you and your students are familiar with and use safety measures and protective gear. One can never be too cautious in these matters.

© Shell Education

Correlation to Standards

The No Child Left Behind (NCLB) legislation mandates that all states adopt academic standards that identify the skills students will learn in kindergarten through grade 12. While many states had already adopted academic standards prior to NCLB, the legislation set requirements to ensure the standards were detailed and comprehensive.

Standards are designed to focus instruction and guide adoption of curricula. Standards are statements that describe the criteria necessary for students to meet specific academic goals. They define the knowledge, skills, and content students should acquire at each level. Standards are also used to develop standardized tests to evaluate students' academic progress.

In many states today, teachers are required to demonstrate how their lessons meet state standards. State standards are used in the development of Shell Education products, so educators can be assured that they meet the academic requirements of each state.

How to Find Your State Correlations

Shell Education is committed to producing educational materials that are research and standards based. In this effort, all products are correlated to the academic standards of the 50 states, the District of Columbia, and the Department of Defense Dependent Schools. A correlation report customized for your state can be printed directly from the following website: **http://www.shelleducation.com**.

If you require assistance in printing correlation reports, please contact Customer Service at 1-800-877-3450.

McREL Compendium

Shell Education uses the *Mid-continent Research for Education and Learning (McREL) Compendium* to create standards correlations. Each year, McREL analyzes state standards and revises the compendium. By following this procedure, they are able to produce a general compilation of national standards.

Each science skill assessed in this book is based on one or more McREL content standards. The charts on the following pages shows the McREL standards that correlate to each lesson used in the book.

Correlation to Standards (cont.)

Standard 2: Understands Earth's composition and structure	
Skill: Knows components of soil and other factors that influence soil texture, fertility, and resistance to erosion	Soil, page 74 Comparing Soils, page 75 Classifying Soil, page 77 Measuring Soil Particle Size, page 78 Measuring Water in Soil, page 79 Measuring Humus in Soil, page 81 Soil and Ultraviolet Light, page 83 Comparing Soil under UV Light, page 84 Acidity Indicators in Soil, page 85 Soil Case Study, page 86 Measuring Soil Acidity, page 87
Standard 4: Understands the principles of heredity and related concepts	
Skill: Knows that hereditary information is contained in genes (located in the chromosomes of each cell)	Hair, page 30 Comparing Hairs, page 32 Blood, page 37 Comparing Blood Samples, page 42 DNA, page 49 Extracting DNA, page 54
Standard 5: Understands the structure and function of cells and organisms	
Skill: Knows that all organisms are composed of cells, which are the fundamental units of life	Hair, page 30 Comparing Hairs, page 32 Blood, page 37 Comparing Blood Samples, page 42 DNA, page 49 Extracting DNA, page 54
Standard 8: Understands the structure and properties of matter	
Skill: Knows methods used to separate mixtures into their component parts (boiling, filtering, chromatography, screening)	All fact sheets and lab activities

© Shell Education

Correlation to Standards (cont.)

Standard 9: Understands the sources and properties of energy	
Skill: Knows ways in which light interacts with matter (e.g., transmission, including refraction; absorption; scattering, including reflection)	Infrared and Ultraviolet Light, page 62 Liquids in UV light, page 64 Spectroscopes, page 65 Spectroscopy, page 67 Soil and Ultraviolet Light, page 83 Comparing Soil under UV Light, page 84
Skill: Knows that only a narrow range of wavelengths of electromagnetic radiation can be seen by the human eye; differences of wavelength within that range of visible light are perceived as differences in color	Infrared and Ultraviolet Light, page 62 Liquids in UV light, page 64 Spectroscopes, page 65 Spectroscopy, page 67
Standard 11: Understands the nature of scientific knowledge	
Skill: Understands the nature of scientific explanations (e.g., use of logically consistent arguments; emphasis on evidence; use of scientific principles, models, and theories; acceptance or displacement of explanations based on new scientific evidence)	What Is Forensic Science?, page 11 Using Forensic Science: Contact Traces, page 28 All fact sheets and lab activities
Standard 12: Understands the nature of scientific inquiry	
Skill: Knows that there is no fixed procedure called "the scientific method," but that investigations involve systematic observations; carefully collected, relevant evidence; logical reasoning; and some imagination in developing hypotheses and explanations	What Is Forensic Science?, page 11 Using Forensic Science: Contact Traces, page 28 All fact sheets and lab activities

Correlation to Standards (cont.)

Standard 12: Understands the nature of scientific inquiry *(cont.)*	
Skill: Designs and conducts a scientific investigation (e.g., formulates hypotheses, designs and executes investigations, interprets data, synthesizes evidence into explanations, proposes alternative explanations for observations, critiques explanations and procedures)	What Is Forensic Science?, page 11 Using Forensic Science: Contact Traces, page 28 All fact sheets and lab activities
Skill: Uses appropriate tools (including computer hardware and software) and techniques to gather, analyze, and interpret scientific data	What Is Forensic Science?, page 11 How to Use Forensic Science: Contact Traces, page 28 All fact sheets and lab activities
Skill: Establishes relationships based on evidence and logical argument (e.g., provides causes for effects)	What Is Forensic Science?, page 11 How to Use Forensic Science: Contact Traces, page 28 All fact sheets and lab activities
Standard 13: Understands the scientific enterprise	
Skill: Knows that the work of science requires a variety of human abilities, qualities, and habits of mind (e.g., reasoning, insight, energy, skill, creativity, intellectual honesty, tolerance of ambiguity, skepticism, openness to new ideas)	What Is Forensic Science?, page 11 How to Use Forensic Science: Contact Traces, page 28 All fact sheets and lab activities
Skill: Knows various settings in which scientists and engineers may work (e.g., colleges and universities, businesses and industries, research institutes, government agencies)	What Is Forensic Science?, page 11 How to Use Forensic Science: Contact Traces, page 28

© Shell Education

What Is Forensic Science?

The word *forensic* comes from the Latin word *forensis*, meaning "connected with the forum." The forum was the Roman square where the Court of Law and public discussions were held. In some countries, such as Canada and the United States, forensic science is also known as criminalistics.

Forensic science is any science that is used to solve crimes, and its results are used in the courts of law. It is based on the belief that whenever a contact is made, there is always some exchange of material. This principle was first suggested by the famous French criminologist Edmond Locard who, in 1910, said that a criminal always leaves something at the scene of a crime, or takes something away. In other words, when a person comes in contact with an object or another person, there is always some material transferred from one to the other. This has been referred to as Locard's Exchange Principle. These pieces of evidence are for the police to find and for the forensic scientist to analyze.

Things left at a crime scene can include fingerprints, small fibers from clothes, body hair, saliva left on a sealed envelope, or other body fluids. A suspect can be incriminated if flakes of their skin are found under the nails of a victim who has been attacked. A criminal may take away drops of a victim's blood, some hair or fibers from the victim's clothes, or soil from the crime scene on the soles of his or her shoes. The expression used today for such exchanged materials is "contact traces" or "trace evidence." Other evidence can include footprints, tire prints from the getaway car, tool marks from a forced entry, ink, paint flakes, and oil. In fact, anything, no matter how small, that has been altered by the crime can be called a contact trace.

What Is Forensic Science? (cont.)

Before the 20th century, criminals had it very easy. As long as there were no witnesses, criminals were hardly ever caught. With modern technology today, however, it is almost impossible to commit the perfect crime. The criminal would have to be naked, have a shaved head and body, wear gloves, and destroy them and all tools afterwards. Even then, there would be no guarantee that there were no traces left behind or carried away from the scene.

Today, eyewitness accounts are still very helpful in bringing a criminal to justice. A car registration number recorded by an eyewitness can lead to a possible suspect and save the police many hours of work. A good description of a criminal by an eyewitness can lead to the speedy capture of a suspect and eliminate other innocent people from police inquiries.

To be a good eyewitness, a person should be alert and observant. In this way, he or she can notice and remember as many details as possible.

Comprehension Questions

1. Explain how forensic science is different from other branches of science.
2. About how long ago do you think that the solving of crimes became a science? Who or what do you think was a major influence on this?
3. Explain why it is more difficult for a criminal to get away with a crime nowadays than it was 100 years ago.
4. How were criminals usually caught before modern forensic science techniques were used to analyze evidence?
5. How can you be a good eyewitness? Give examples.
6. Copy Locard's Exchange Principle and explain what it means.
7. Why is a knife used in an assault not always a contact trace?
8. Explain why contact trace evidence is so important in solving crimes.

© Shell Education

What Is Forensic Science? (cont.)

How Observant Are You?

Below is a scene that could be in any suburban street. Look at it for 30 seconds. Then turn over the page and answer the questions from the next page.

What Is Forensic Science? (cont.)

Comprehension Questions

1. How many vehicles are in the picture?
2. How many children are in the picture? What are they doing?
3. How many people are in the car? Describe them in as much detail as you can.
4. What type of car is it? Is there anything different about the car?
5. What is the man on the other side of the road doing?
6. How would you describe the location of the scene?
7. Describe the parked car.
8. What can you recall about the houses on the street?
9. Are there any animals in the picture? If so, how many, and what are they doing?
10. Can you remember anything else about the picture?

Look back at the picture and mark every answer that was correct. How did you do? Would you make a good police witness?

This exercise depends on careful observation and an accurate memory. Unfortunately, when most crimes are committed, witnesses are not expecting anything and are caught unawares. A witness may not even realize a crime is taking place until some time afterwards. However, many offenders have been caught thanks to accurate eyewitness accounts. Good witnesses can lead to possible suspects, or they may help the police investigators look in the right place for possible clues.

Now, without looking at the picture again, try to answer the following question.

11. Imagine you observed the scene on the previous page as an eyewitness. A few minutes after this scene took place, a police car drove up, and the police told you that they were chasing some people they believe may have taken part in robbing a bank. The robbery happened a few minutes ago back along the street. Make a list of at least five separate pieces of information that you saw that might help the police to find who was involved.

© Shell Education

Looking for Differences

To be a good detective or forensic scientist, you must have good observation skills and be able to detect small differences and objects out of place.

Comprehension Question

Look carefully at the two pictures drawn above. In your notebook, write as many differences as you can find. You should be able to find about 15.

Score

- Less than 4 – keep trying
- Over 4 – not bad for a newcomer to forensics
- Over 8 – good detective work
- Over 12 – brilliant work

What Is Forensic Science? (cont.)

Arriving at the Crime Scene

Even the best experts in the world cannot solve a crime without evidence. Therefore, it is essential that the scene of the crime be treated in the correct way.

A. Securing the Crime Scene

In most cases the first police officer on the scene will be a uniformed police officer. They are not usually trained as detectives and should touch as little as possible of the crime scene and the area in the vicinity.

All precautions should be taken to avoid any accidental destruction or contamination of potential evidence.

The officer who arrives on the scene first will ensure the safety of any injured people and of the site itself. This may involve turning off gas, water, and electricity supplies. Ideally, the site should be secured with a physical barrier so that no unauthorized people can enter. This will leave the site as close as possible to the state it was in at the time of the crime, preserving all traces left by the criminals for the officers trained in searching for evidence.

When it is obvious that a person is dead, the body is not touched or moved in any way until it has been carefully examined and photographed. If there are injured people involved, the police officer will see to their safety and call an ambulance before doing anything else.

While waiting, the uniformed officer may record the names and addresses of any eyewitnesses to the crime.

B. Examining the Scene

If a major crime has been committed, then the next person on the scene will probably be the senior detective in charge of the investigation. A police surgeon and/or a pathologist may be called in if a body is involved.

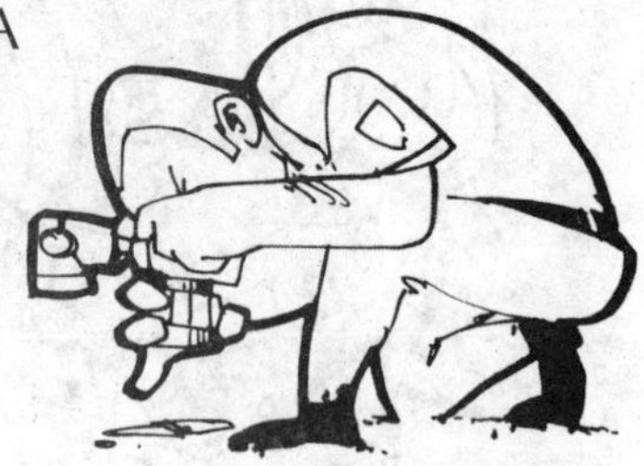

Specially trained crime scene investigators (CSIs), also called scene of crime officers (SOCOs), who are experts at looking for evidence, are called in at an early stage of the investigation.

A police photographer, or a CSI experienced in photography, will take pictures (still photos and possibly videos) of any victim and the positions of the body. Wounds or other medical features that could help future investigations may also be photographed.

Photographs or videos will be taken to help a court understand the crime. Because the court cannot see the scene as the police investigator saw it, an oral description with photographs and video is the next best option available.

© Shell Education

What Is Forensic Science? (cont.)

Arriving at the Crime Science (cont.)

Such a detailed description may even save money and time if it saves the court the necessity of visiting the site.

Photographs make a visible record while the evidence is fresh and undisturbed. They should be taken from all angles to provide an objective and accurate record of how the scene was left by the criminal. On some occasions, photographs have revealed evidence that was not noticed when the scene was first searched.

To help record the actual size of an object being photographed, a ruler marked with a suitable scale is usually included in the photo. If photographs of a crime scene are taken from where an eyewitness was standing, they can be most useful later when the witness's statement is evaluated. The photo can confirm that the witness could really have seen what he or she claimed to have seen.

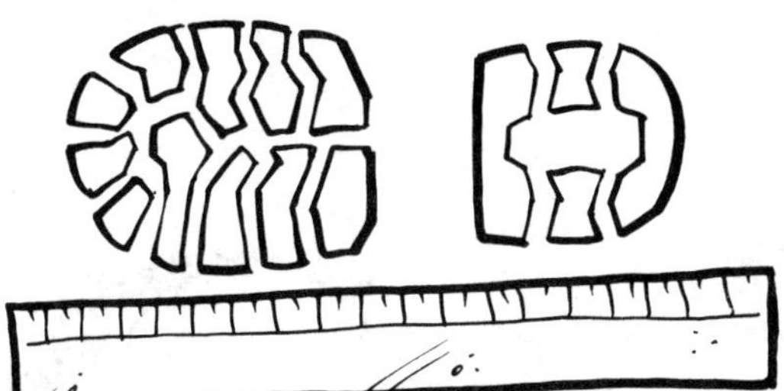

A police draftsperson may be asked to sketch plans of the site. On this map, vital information is recorded. Such information may include the position of doors, windows, and furniture; the exact measurements of distances, heights, and angles; and the positions of bloodstains, weapons, and other evidence.

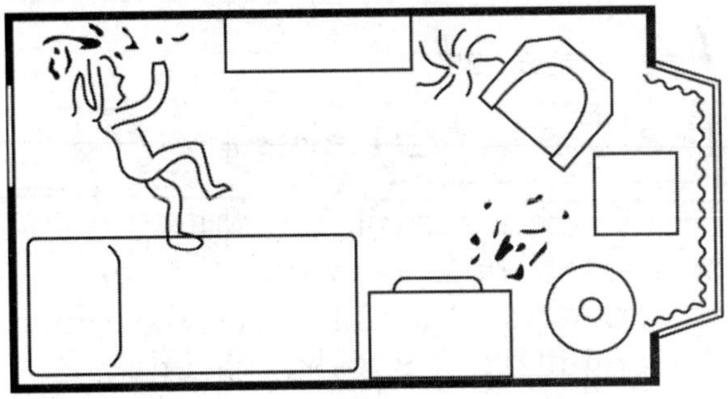

A thorough search often takes several hours, and if it includes a large outdoor area, it can even take days or weeks. In such cases, police or army cadets may be called in and, after an initial briefing about what to look for, they are able to cover a large area very thoroughly.

To avoid contamination, the CSIs put on special overalls and overshoes before starting work. This is to avoid leaving any traces themselves at the scene. They usually try to approach the site using the same route as the first police officer on the scene. On some occasions, boardwalks or platforms are used to approach the scene in order to minimize any interference.

Usually the immediate area surrounding the scene is searched thoroughly first. Things like foot and tire prints are very perishable and so must be collected as quickly as possible before they are lost to bad weather or accidental damage.

What Is Forensic Science? (cont.)

Arriving at the Crime Scene (cont.)

If the crime scene is in a building, the next area to be inspected will be the point of entry. The CSI must try to think as a criminal might and predict the movements the criminal probably made, so that he or she will be able to identify the most likely places where evidence may be found and look there first. For example, they may look for fibers from clothes on a door frame at shoulder height where the criminal may have rubbed his or her shoulder.

It is the CSI's role to assess the crime scene and prioritize how it will be searched. Often, the actual crime scene is searched last. The CSI may call in extra expert help, such as a pathologist, to examine a dead body; a forensic biologist to analyze blood splatters; or a ballistics expert to look at powder burns or inspect some discarded cartridge cases.

Only after the CSI is satisfied that all possible evidence has been collected will the cleanup of the site begin. Bodies will be removed to the morgue where a police pathologist will make a postmortem examination. All other pieces of evidence are photographed before their positions at the crime scene are recorded on a map. They will then be collected, bagged, and labeled before being sent to the laboratory, where they will undergo the appropriate analysis as requested by the officer in charge of the investigation.

Comprehension Questions

1. In the correct order, list four things that should be done by the first police officer who arrives at a major crime scene. Give reasons for your answer.
2. Explain the difference between the roles of the crime scene investigator and the detective in charge of the investigation.
3. Describe at least three procedures that are carried out to prevent contamination of the crime scene.
4. Explain why in most serious crimes a large number of photographs are taken and a map drawn.
5. Why is a small ruler placed in a photograph of a piece of evidence?
6. When would a forensic pathologist be called in, and what is his or her responsibility?

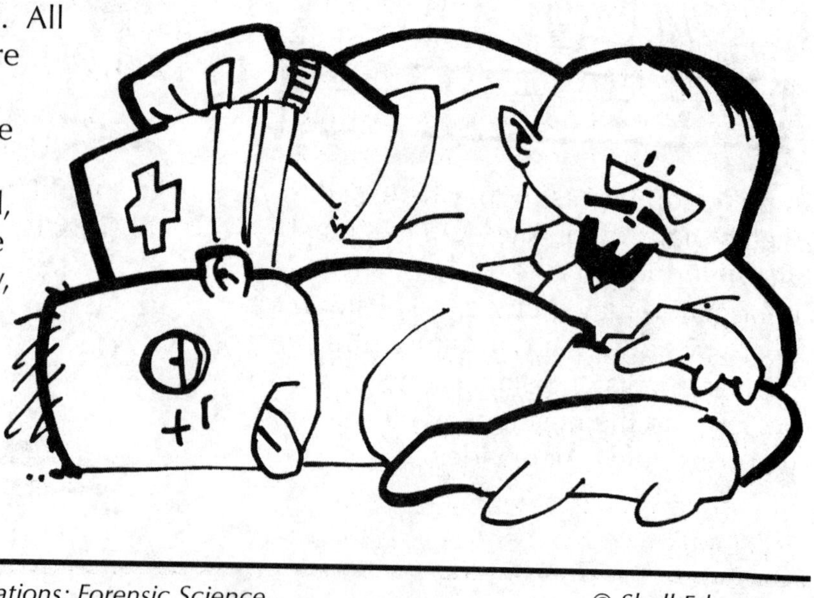

© Shell Education

Removing the Evidence

The evidence from the crime scene must be transported to the forensic laboratory very carefully and systematically so that no evidence is lost, misplaced, or damaged in any way. To prevent cross-contamination from the crime scene, investigators wear special overalls and overshoes. Locations associated with a possible suspect are usually searched by different crime scene investigators (CSIs) other than those who searched the crime scene, and any evidence is transported by different vehicles to avoid contamination.

Sometimes in court a defense lawyer may challenge the prosecution, suggesting that an item of evidence tendered in court is not the same as the item that left the crime scene. The lawyer may try to make the members of the jury suspect a possible gap in the chain of continuity in the handling of a particular item. The lawyer may raise the possibility of cross-contamination. To prevent a case from being lost, all care must be taken to ensure the validity of the evidence.

At the crime scene, all items of possible evidence are labeled and sealed in bags where possible. The label records the location where the item was found, the date and time found, and the name of the police officer handing the item over. A laboratory registration number is added at the forensic laboratory to record all details, including the time of arrival at the laboratory.

This information is entered into a register that has a separate entry for each item to record all movement of the item and by whom, while in the laboratory. This register can be used in court if the chain of continuity is challenged by the defense lawyers.

Comprehension Questions

1. Explain why CSIs wear special overalls and overshoes while at the crime scene.
2. Why do you think it is usual for one CSI to search a suspect's house and another to search the crime scene?
3. Explain why every item of evidence that is removed from the crime scene is enclosed in its own carefully labeled plastic bag.

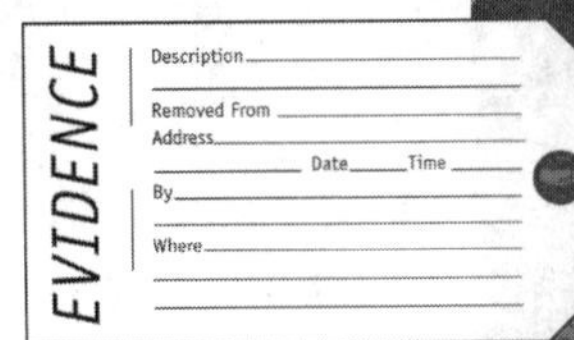

EVIDENCE

Description ____
Removed From ____
Address ____
____ Date ____ Time ____
By ____
Where ____

4. What information is recorded on the outside of the evidence bag?

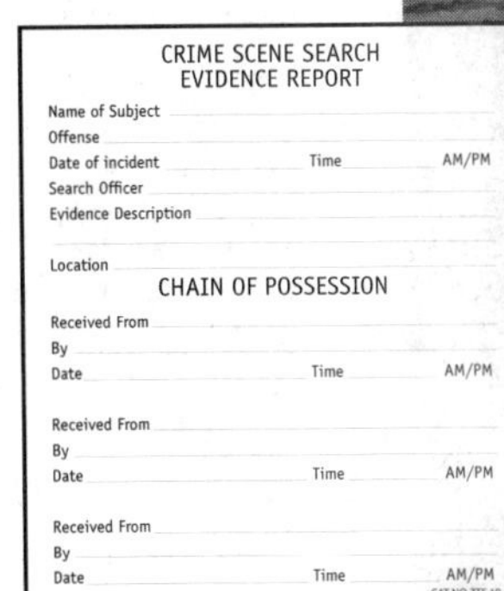

CRIME SCENE SEARCH
EVIDENCE REPORT

Name of Subject ____
Offense ____
Date of incident ____ Time ____ AM/PM
Search Officer ____
Evidence Description ____
Location ____

CHAIN OF POSSESSION

Received From ____
By ____
Date ____ Time ____ AM/PM

Received From ____
By ____
Date ____ Time ____ AM/PM

Received From ____
By ____
Date ____ Time ____ AM/PM

CAT NO ZTE 10

5. Describe what happens to the evidence once it arrives at the forensic laboratory.
6. Why is it so important to prevent cross-contamination?
7. Below is a tag that was attached to an item of evidence when it arrived at the forensic laboratory. What important information needs to be added?

BURGLARY
at
25 High St, Smithton
Found behind the sofa

PC Jones

What Is Forensic Science? (cont.)

The Forensic Science Laboratory

The forensic scientist, employed full-time by the police department, is the analyst back in the laboratory. He or she usually does not visit the crime scene. The forensic scientist's main responsibility is to help the police investigation by using his or her specialized knowledge and techniques. Forensic scientists usually have a science degree from a university, with specialized training and experience on top of that. They are often not police officers, and they do not usually interview witnesses or suspects; interviewing is left to the police officers.

Many forensic scientists specialize in a certain area of forensics such as fingerprint identification, DNA profiling, or forgery detection. It is the forensic scientist who can identify whether a hair is human or animal and can identify from what part of the body it came. A forensic scientist who specializes in ballistics can often identify the exact gun from which a bullet was fired.

The forensic laboratory houses many pieces of expensive and specialized equipment to help the scientist analyze the evidence. Once an item arrives at the laboratory, the forensic scientist decides which tests or analyses it should undergo, and in what order. Some tests will destroy part or all of the evidence, while other tests will not affect the sample at all. Obviously, all nondestructive tests should be carried out first. The scientist needs to know the information required by the investigating officers in order to select the appropriate tests.

To prevent cross-contamination in the laboratory, all evidence from the crime scene is stored in a different place from any items taken from a suspect's home or car. Items from the different scenes are analyzed by different forensic scientists where possible, and always on different days and in different rooms.

© Shell Education

The Forensic Science Laboratory (cont.)

Other experts may be called in to analyze specific evidence or give their opinion on some matter in which they have expertise—perhaps a practicing dentist or dental technician who has expertise in identifying a person from dental records, or a psychologist who can draw up a profile of a serial killer. Their role in court is exactly the same as a person who is employed full-time as a forensic scientist. Such people are called expert witnesses.

Comprehension Questions

1. What would the following experts specialize in? Discuss the types of cases about which they may be asked to testify.
   a. dentist
   b. psychologist
   c. entymologist
   d. serologist
   e. pathologist
2. How may a forensic scientist differ from an expert witness, if at all?
3. How does the role of the crime scene investigator differ from that of the forensic scientist?
4. An unusual red fiber was found caught on the clothes of a victim of an assault. Not long afterwards, a suspect wearing a red sweater of a similar color was brought in for questioning. Some samples of the fibers were removed from the suspect's sweater and taken to the forensic laboratory for testing. It was decided to test the fibers for strength by placing each of them in a clamp and then pulling and measuring at what force the fiber broke. A melting test was also done, to determine at what temperature the fiber would melt. The fibers were examined under the microscope and their colors were compared under ultraviolet light. Discuss the order in which the tests should have been carried out and why they should be done in this order.
5. If the two fibers mentioned in question number four had the same melting point, strength, and thickness, and appeared the same under natural and ultraviolet light, what conclusion can you come to regarding the source of the two fibers and the guilt of the suspect?

What Is Forensic Science? (cont.)

Going to Trial

In court, the suspect, the person who the police believe carried out the crime, is put on trial before a judge and jury. It is often the quality of the police evidence that will influence the opinion of both the jury and the judge.

In a jury trial, the judge is there to listen and pass a sentence if the jury decides that the accused is guilty. The prosecution lawyer puts forward the police case and calls any expert witnesses to give his or her opinion in order to convince the jury of the facts of the case.

The defense lawyer must try to defend the person charged with the crime by trying to point out any holes in the prosecution's argument and to try to put doubt in the jury members' minds. Only the jury can decide if the accused is guilty or not, beyond any reasonable doubt. An expert witness may also be called in by the defense to discredit the case against a suspect.

The scientific evidence must be presented in a way that can be understood by the court, and not in a way that may confuse it. Judges, lawyers, and juries do not usually have a deep knowledge of science, so all scientific results have to be presented in nontechnical terms. This is why photographs, videos, maps, and plaster casts are so important.

Because of the court's lack of scientific expertise, the forensic scientist or expert witness must be prepared to give an expert opinion on what the evidence implies—that is, he or she must be able to say how likely it is that the crime is linked to the suspect who has been charged. The scientist may give an opinion of the probability of the soil found on the suspect's shoe coming from the crime scene, or the suspect's fingerprint matching one found on some stolen property, hence linking the suspect to the crime.

The forensic scientist not only needs to be qualified and experienced in his or her field of expertise, but also needs to be accepted by the court as having a reliable expert opinion. The court will want to know the extent to which the scientist has specialized in the process under question, and how well the person keeps up-to-date with developments in his or her field. The court will question any previous experience in similar investigations and the number of times the scientist has been permitted to offer expert evidence at other trials.

Comprehension Questions

1. Who decides if the suspect being charged is guilty or innocent?
2. What is the role of the judge in a court of law?
3. Describe the defense lawyer's job and how it differs from that of the prosecution lawyer.
4. What is the role of the expert witness at court?
5. How should scientific evidence be presented in court so that a nonscientific jury easily understands it?
6. Describe several techniques used by forensic scientists to show a nonscientific jury exactly what scientists believe occurred at the scene of a crime.

 © Shell Education

Comprehension Questions (cont.)

7. What does a scientist need in order to be accepted as an expert witness at a trial?

8. Who might be called as an expert witness to give an opinion to a court?

9. Why is the expert witness's opinion necessary?

Microscopes in the Forensic Laboratory

The microscope is still one of the most commonly used and important tools in the forensic laboratory. The simplest microscope is a magnifying lens that has been used for over 100 years to examine anything from fingerprints to footprints. It can magnify objects 10 to 20 times their actual size.

The common compound microscope found in many schools is another useful but relatively inexpensive piece of equipment used regularly in the forensic laboratory. It is used when a magnification of up to 1,000 times is needed. It has two lenses: an eyepiece lens at the top through which the scientist looks, and an objective lens at the lower end of the barrel, near the object being examined. Most compound microscopes have three or four objective lenses of different powers of magnification that can be selected by rotating them. Hairs, fibers, glass fragments, pollen grains, and fingerprint samples are all commonly examined under such a microscope.

If even greater magnification is required, then an electron microscope may be used. Relying on a beam of electrons rather than visible light, this instrument can give images of molecules and even atoms. It can magnify up to 200,000 times and can be used to examine soil, bacteria, or pollen grains to show the smallest differences. Generally, these instruments are not found in a forensic laboratory, so scientists must send material away to be examined under an electron microscope if they believe that it will reveal important information.

The stereoscopic microscope is also a very useful instrument in the forensic laboratory. It has two eyepiece lenses that allow objects to be seen in three dimensions. It has a quite low magnification of about 50 to 100 times, but allows specimens such as soil, hair, and fibers that have been collected to be sorted for closer inspection under other microscopes of higher magnification. Quite large objects can be inspected, such as a small paint chip from a car that can be placed vertically in modeling clay so that all the layers can be examined.

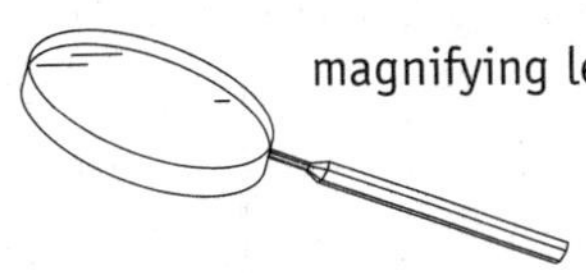
magnifying lens

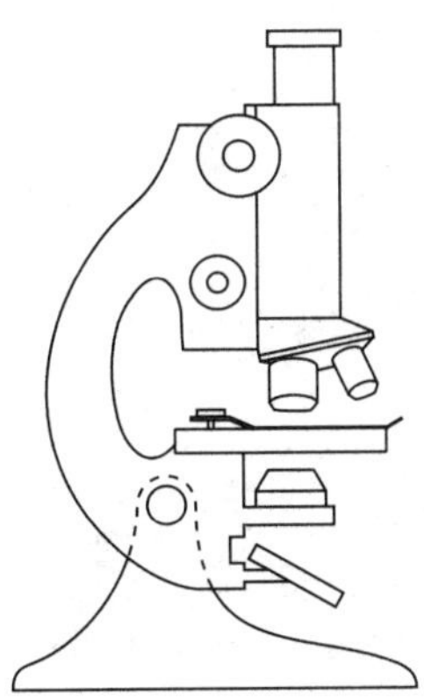
compound microscope

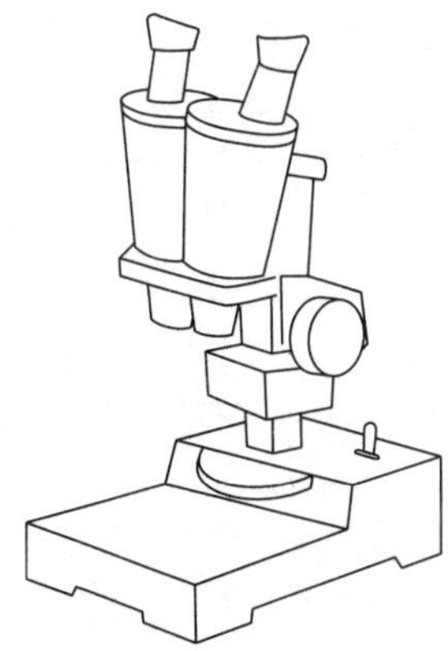
stereoscopic microscope

What Is Forensic Science? (cont.)

Microscopes in the Forensic Laboratory (cont.)

An unusual microscope that is commonly found in the forensic laboratory is the comparison microscope. It is really two microscopes in one, and it is used to compare two different objects at the same time. Its magnification is lower (from five times to about 40 times) than that which is possible with the compound microscope. However, it allows the user to adjust the focus of each object separately so that they are viewed through the one eyepiece lens as two halves of one object. Objects most commonly compared in this way are hairs or fibers, fingerprints, and marks on bullets. One specimen would be from the crime scene and the other from a suspect or a test firing using a known gun. It was for this latter use that this instrument was invented in the United States in the 1920s.

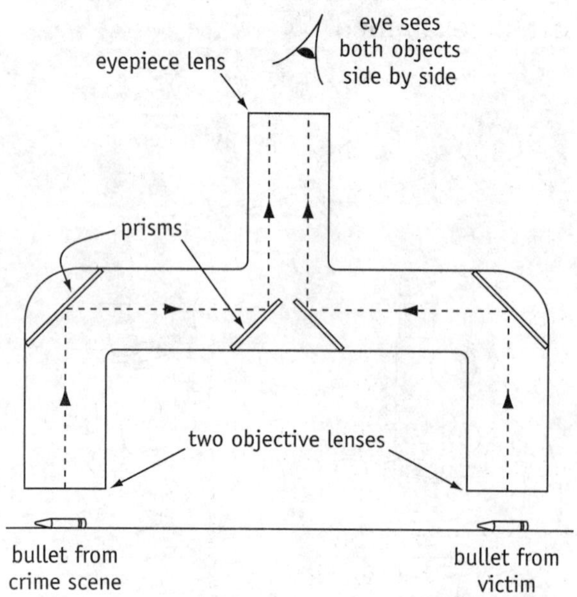

How the comparison microscope works

A forensic scientist using a comparison microscope

Comprehension Questions

1. Why do you think a microscope is such an important instrument in the forensic laboratory?
2. Which type of microscope was invented specifically for use in forensic science? Explain why it was invented.
3. Which type of microscope is least likely to be found in a small forensic laboratory? Explain why.
4. Write a summary of the five types of microscopes from this and the previous page, mentioning how each is used in solving crimes.

 © Shell Education

A Crime Scenario: Theft at Hilltop Farm

The old green car stopped at the gate while the driver checked the name. "Hilltop Farm" was painted on the gate, so the driver turned in and drove slowly up the drive. The surface was covered mainly in gravel, but as the car rounded the bend near the house, the driver felt the back wheels slip slightly as they went through a patch of mud on the driveway.

He could see the house now. It was in darkness, so his information was correct. The owners had gone away for a few days, taking their dogs. There was no alarm system either, his informant had said. This was a burglar's dream. He stopped the car at the side of the house, out of sight of the drive, and crept towards the nearest window. It was nicely visible in the moonlight.

He stepped onto the garden to take a look at the window latch. He brushed the flowering acacia tree as he tried to get a better look. He was in luck—there was no lock. He attempted to lever open the window with a large screwdriver he had brought with him just for this job. Unfortunately, the window was jammed; so, using the back of the screwdriver, he gave the glass a sharp tap. It broke easily. He removed the large jagged pieces and climbed through into a lounge room, ripping his jacket as he did so.

As he put his hand on the back of the chair near the window, he realized that his hand was bleeding. He must have cut himself on the glass. He wrapped his handkerchief around the wound to stop the bleeding. He would see to it later.

He turned on his flashlight and was a bit startled to see a pair of cat's eyes staring at him from the chair near the door. Obviously, someone would be coming in to feed it. He hoped that it would be much later, but better not make too much mess, and hopefully his crime would not be noticed until the owners returned in a couple of days. At least cats don't bark.

He moved towards the desk and started searching through the drawers. He found a few coins, a medal, and a small brooch that he put in his pocket. His eyes lit up when he saw the checkbook. There was one cash check, made out for only $5. The signature was there too, but it was not an easy one to copy. However, there would be enough room between the two words to add the word "hundred" and to add two zeros after the number five in the figures. He would try to cash it before the owners came back from their vacation.

Suddenly, he thought he heard a car. He quickly turned off his flashlight and could see car headlights coming up the drive. He could feel the sweat on his hands and the hair standing up on the back of his neck.

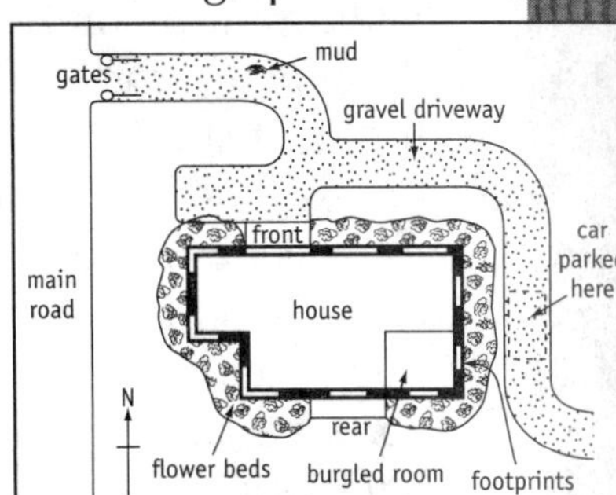

He moved across to the window, steadying himself on the table as he went. He tripped over the cat and fell into the chair where it had been sitting. He stood up quickly and climbed out the window. He reached his car just as a key turned in the lock of the front door.

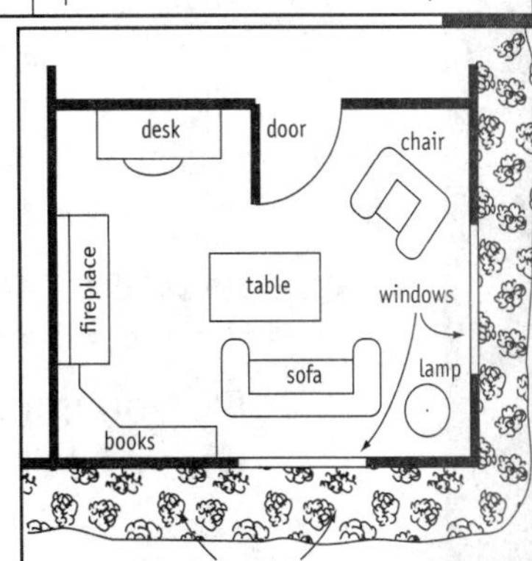

What Is Forensic Science? (cont.)

A Crime Scenario (cont.)

Without turning on his lights, the thief was able to roll down the drive before turning on his engine and then driving away in the dark. The moonlight was a great help, but it disappeared behind a cloud as he neared the gate. He felt a bump and heard a crunching noise as his car scraped against the gate.

He flipped on his headlights as he turned onto the road. They worked, but he supposed he would be left with a dent and possibly a broken light. As he drove, the oil warning light began to glow on the dashboard. His engine had been losing oil lately, and he had meant to fix that. He was relieved to see that he was not being followed.

The next day, after changing the check to $500, he went to the bank. He felt nervous, though he was sure the family wouldn't have missed the check yet. But when a policeman entered the bank, he panicked and ran off.

Without looking back, he walked quickly around the corner and entered the next shop, which he knew had a back entrance to the alley and parking lot. As he passed through the shop, he took off the navy coat that he had been wearing, and dropped it into the garbage can that was placed beside the back door. He now wore a pale blue windbreaker that he was sure would not link him to the bank or the crime at Hilltop Farm. He felt quite safe now.

Comprehension Questions

1. Do you think the thief got away with it? Why do you think this?
2. Make a list of the clues the thief left behind. There are at least 10. Next to each item, write what you think the crime scene investigator will do with these clues.
3. Can you think of any contact traces that the thief may have unwittingly carried away from the crime scene that could link him to the crime? Make a list of all the things you can think of. Explain how the police could use them as evidence.
4. Describe any other evidence, other than trace evidence, that may link the thief to the crime scene.
5. Once the police bring in the thief to the police station to question him as a possible suspect, what questions do you think they would ask him?
6. Which of the suspect's belongings might the police ask to inspect? Why do you think this?
7. What type of police officer do you think may have been the first called to the scene, and what do you think this person would do there?
8. Which specialist police officers might have been called to the scene? What would be their task?
9. Describe some of the things the thief may say when being questioned to try to explain away some of the evidence and maintain his innocence.
10. Which evidence do you think the thief will find hardest to explain? Give reasons for your answer.

© Shell Education

What Is Forensic Science? (cont.)

Forensic Science Word Search

Look carefully at the grid and find the words listed below. When complete, there should be 24 letters remaining. These letters spell out a sentence that is the basic principle of forensic science.

E	D	R	A	C	O	L	D	N	O	M	D	E	V	C
L	Y	F	I	N	G	E	R	P	R	I	N	T	S	R
I	G	E	O	E	C	N	E	D	I	V	E	I	S	I
O	O	T	C	R	I	M	E	S	C	E	N	E	E	M
R	L	H	S	Y	E	B	C	G	O	V	N	X	N	I
F	O	E	T	I	L	N	N	A	E	G	T	P	T	N
O	C	F	C	O	G	I	S	S	T	L	E	E	I	A
R	I	T	O	L	K	O	T	I	E	A	L	R	W	L
G	X	D	A	A	V	I	L	S	C	S	L	T	T	I
E	O	E	E	S	G	A	T	O	Y	S	U	I	R	S
R	T	R	R	A	S	R	I	A	H	L	B	S	U	T
I	B	A	T	R	E	D	R	U	M	T	A	E	O	I
E	P	O	C	S	O	R	C	I	M	C	A	N	C	C
S	R	N	O	I	S	S	E	R	P	M	I	P	A	S
E	B	A	L	L	I	S	T	I	C	S	T	S	A	C

1. analyst
2. ballistics
3. blood
4. breaking
5. bullet
6. cast
7. court
8. forensic
9. forgeries
10. glass
11. hairs
12. impression
13. investigator
14. microscope
15. crime scene
16. criminalistics
17. Edmond Locard
18. evidence
19. expertise
20. fingerprints
21. murder
22. oil
23. pathologist
24. theft
25. toxicology
26. witness

Basic principle of forensic science:

_ _ _ _ _

_ _ _ _ _ _ _

_ _ _ _ _ _

_   _ _ _ _ _.

Using Forensic Science: Contact Traces

In 1910, the French criminologist Edmond Locard proposed his "Exchange Principle." He stated that "every contact leaves a trace." The traces he was talking about include fingerprints, hairs, fibers, glass and paint fragments, and even pollens.

We constantly drop hair from our bodies and shed fibers from our clothes. If there is a cat or a dog in our home, its fur can be transferred onto our clothes and carried to a new location. Pollens from plants around our home or workplace can land on our clothes and be carried away to be deposited at another site. A burglar who breaks a window to enter a building is often showered with minute fragments of glass that can get caught in the seams and pockets of clothing. All these very small items of evidence are referred to as contact traces or trace evidence, and will be meticulously searched for by the CSIs. It is almost impossible for a criminal and a victim to be in contact and not exchange particles of some sort. This exchange principle is the basis of all modern forensic science, with the particles that are exchanged being the key to solving the crime.

Searching for Trace Evidence

At a crime scene, after the large, easily seen objects like weapons and clothes have been removed, the area may be vacuumed so that all loose threads, hair, and other small trace particles will be caught in a special container called a vacuum trap. Before moving a dead body to the mortuary where the postmortem will be carried out, the forensic pathologist wraps the head, hands, and feet in separate plastic bags so that no small traces may drop off and be lost before a thorough inspection can be made. Any debris under the fingernails from a possible struggle could also yield important evidence, as could any foreign particles that have been breathed into the air passages.

The CSIs may press a type of sticky tape all over the victim's clothes, the carpets, curtains, and sofas to collect any loose fibers or hairs. Sometimes, clothes are shaken or beaten above a large funnel in the forensic laboratory examination room so that any loose fibers, hairs, pollens, glass, or other particles that may have become attached to the garments can be collected. They are then bagged and labeled before being sent to the forensic laboratory to be examined under a stereoscopic microscope. Any particles that are present in particularly high numbers are given very close attention. Why would this be so?

The stereoscopic microscope is a very versatile and frequently used instrument. Because its focus is very flexible, it is extremely useful for sorting through debris from a crime scene to locate possible contact traces. The big distance between the stage holding the specimens and the objective lens means that it can be used for quite large objects. Its magnifying power ranges from 50 to 100 times, which is quite low compared to the conventional compound microscope, which ranges from 4 times to 1,000 times, but this low magnification is quite sufficient for sorting.

Comprehension Questions

1. List four examples of a contact trace. Explain how each could be used in helping to solve a crime.
2. Describe three ways in which contact traces can be collected from the crime scene, and explain how they are treated once they are collected.
3. Explain why the stereoscopic microscope is the most suitable instrument for sorting through fine debris from a crime scene.
4. How is a dead body prepared for transport from the crime scene? Why is it done this way?
5. Where would a thorough inspection of a body be made, and by whom is it carried out? Describe the type of trace evidence that person is looking for.

Hair

Although hair cannot usually identify a single individual as fingerprints can, hair found at a crime scene can be very useful. Besides giving some indication of age, race, and sex, hairs found at a crime scene can strengthen the links between a suspect and that scene.

Human hair can be classified into six groups, according to its origin:

- Hair from the scalp tends to have a circular cross-section, often with somewhat split ends.
- Beard hair often has a more triangular cross-section.
- Eyebrows and eyelashes also have a circular cross-section, but their ends are tapered.
- Underarm hair has a more oval cross-section than the other types.
- Pubic hair is often short, curly, and stiff, with an oval or triangular cross-section and short roots.
- General body hair is finer and softer than pubic hair, but is also curly and either triangular or oval in cross-section.

Hair is composed mainly of the protein keratin, which is very difficult to destroy except by fire and certain chemicals. It will remain preserved in the grave longer than most of the body except for the bones. Microscopic inspection of hair can also indicate whether hair was pulled out, cut off, or just fell out naturally.

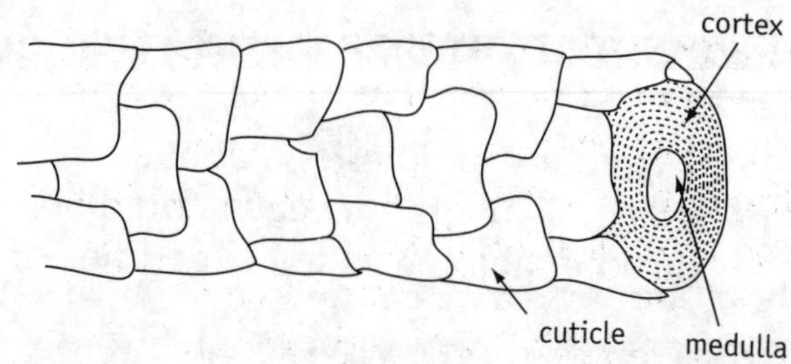

Every person's hair is also unique in the trace elements it contains. These chemicals reflect the food you eat, your work and home environment, and any drugs and poisons you may have consumed as well as the shampoos and other chemicals like dyes and bleaches that you may have put on your hair. In the 1960s, when some of Napoleon's hair was obtained and analyzed more than 100 years after his death, it was found to contain many more times the normal amount of arsenic. In his day arsenic was thought to improve the complexion, but it was also a favorite method of poisoning as its taste was difficult to detect.

A strand of hair consists of three layers:

1. the central core, called the medulla
2. the colored layer, called the cortex, surrounding the medulla
3. the outer layer of overlapping scales, called the cuticle

 © Shell Education

Hair (cont.)

Examination of all three layers can help the forensic scientist to identify the hair. The pattern of overlapping scales in the cuticle is very useful in identifying the type of animal it came from. The medulla, which can vary markedly in different people and animals, can be classified into three groups. (See the diagram to the right).

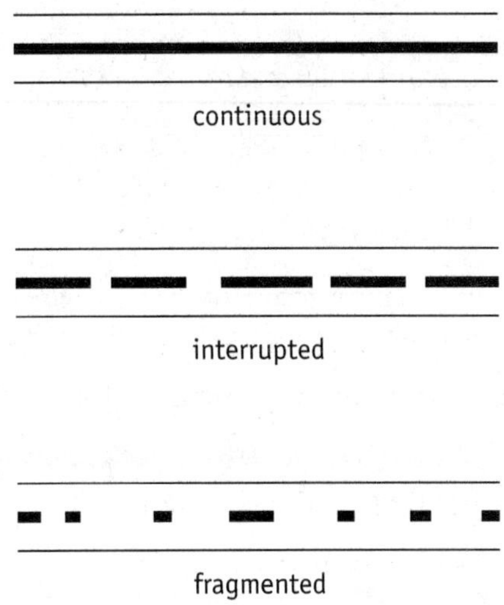

In some humans the medulla may be absent, but the most common is a fragmented medulla. Humans from Asia tend to have a continuous medulla. It is usually cylindrical in shape in humans, but this is not true for many animals. For example, the medulla in cat hair is like a string of pearls.

Comprehension Questions

1. Write a paragraph explaining all the information that might be gained about a person whose hair was found at a crime scene.
2. What are the six parts of the human body that have hair with different characteristics?
3. Of what substance is hair made? How durable is this substance?
4. Name the three layers of a strand of hair, and describe where each is found.
5. What information can a forensic scientist find by inspecting the medulla of a hair sample?
6. How can inspection of the cuticle help in identifying hair?

Name ______________________________

Comparing Hairs

In this activity, you will inspect a number of labeled slides of different hairs under the microscope. You will then use the labeled slides to help you identify some unknown hairs.

Materials

- normal compound microscope
- labeled, prepared slides of some different hairs from different parts of the human body as well as some common animal hairs
- some slides of unknown hairs

Procedure

1. In your science notebook, under the heading "Looking at Hairs," draw the following table:

Type of Hair	**Description**
Unknown 1	
Unknown 2	

2. Look at each hair under the microscope, then write down a description of its appearance in the right-hand column of the table.
3. Using the information you gained from examining the known hairs, try to identify the unknown hairs. Were they human or animal? If human, what part of the body? If animal, what type of animal?

© Shell Education

Name ______________________

Comparing Hairs (cont.)

Analysis

1. What differences did you notice in the hairs from different parts of the body?
2. How did the animal hairs differ from the human hairs?
3. Where do you think the unknown hairs came from? How difficult was it to identify them?
4. What features on the hairs enabled you to tell where each had come from?
5. Look at the diagrams below of the medullas of three different animals and that of a human, magnified 450 times. Try to identify where the hair found at the crime scene came from.

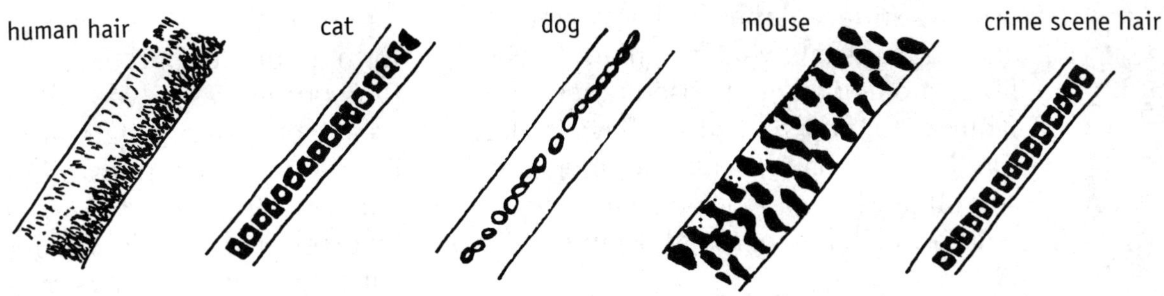

Fibers

If loose fibers found at the crime scene have not come from the victim, they may have come from a large number of sources—from the perpetrator's clothes, from carpet or curtains where the crime occurred, or even from a rug or blanket in which the body was wrapped for transportation, if the body was moved. Also, fibers from the victim may have been deposited on the perpetrator, and these will be looked for on all suspects. Any such fibers found could connect the suspect with the crime scene.

Fibers can be either synthetic (man-made), such as nylon, rayon, polyester, terylene; or they can be natural, being made from either plants (cotton and linen) or from animals (wool, silk, and mohair). Generally, under the microscope, natural fibers have a rougher surface, taper from root to tip, and appear somewhat irregular. Cotton fibers are actually collapsed tubes, while wool fibers, like hair, have scales. On the other hand, synthetic fibers are smooth and even. They also tend to have a much longer length (staple).

linen

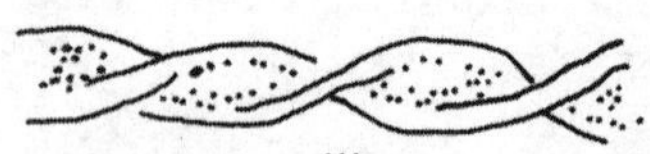

silk

cotton

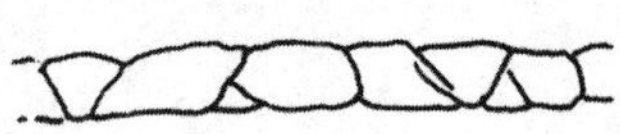

wool

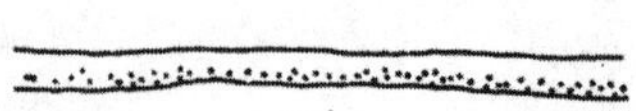

nylon

Fibers of the same type may vary in thickness, depending on how they are made. Their strengths can also vary. Often, both the strengths and thicknesses of any fibers found at a crime scene are measured in the forensic laboratory and compared with any found on a suspect. The melting point of a synthetic fiber is usually measured and its color analyzed. If two fibers look the same under the microscope and have the same thickness, strength, color, and melting point, then they probably both came from the same source. If the fibers are uncommon, then two matching fibers are even more likely to have come from the same garment.

Sometimes, CSIs are fortunate enough to find a piece of fabric instead of only a few fibers. Knitting and weaving can form a number of different patterns. One crime was solved when the weave pattern of a garment was found imprinted on soft putty around a broken window. In another case, a driver involved in a hit-and-run accident was caught when the weave of the victim's clothes left its pattern on the greasy surface of the car's bumper.

The distinctive shape of a piece of fabric found at a crime scene may be compared with the suspect's clothes. If a hole of the same shape and size is found, it will show that the fabric fragment came from that particular garment.

© Shell Education

Fibers (cont.)

Comprehension Questions

1. Explain how fibers can be important evidence in the solving of a crime.

2. Make a sketch of the fibers below. Describe the differences between natural and synthetic fibers.

3. Using the library, try to find the names of at least 12 different fibers: four obtained from animals, four from plants, and four synthetic. If possible, make a sketch of their appearances. Also, try to find out how one of the synthetic fibers is made, and describe the process.

4. Explain at least two ways in which a small piece of fabric found at a crime scene might be useful in solving a crime.

Name ______________________________

Comparing Fibers

In this activity, you will examine the appearance of some different types of fibers on labeled slides under the microscope. You will then use these to identify two unknown fibers.

Materials

- normal compound microscope
- prepared and labeled slides of a number of different fibers
- two slides of some unknown fibers

Procedure

1. In your science notebook, under the heading "Looking at Fibers," create the following table. There should be a separate box for each slide that you examine.

Natural Fibers	wool	cotton	linen	silk
Synthetic Fibers	rayon	polyester	nylon	terylene

2. Inspect the named slides and make a simple sketch of each type in the table.
3. Now look at the two unknown fibers and, using the sketches of the named fibers, identify the type of each fiber, and say whether you think it is natural or synthetic.

Analysis

1. Describe the main differences in the appearance of synthetic fibers and natural fibers.
2. What type of fiber do you think the unknown fibers were? Explain what led you to make this identification.
3. What are three other tests that could be carried out to confirm your identification?
4. Describe a crime scene where fibers would be important forensic evidence.
5. Name five fibers that are not mentioned in this activity. For each one, state whether it is a natural or synthetic fiber.

© Shell Education

Blood

Blood is probably the most important fluid that the forensic biologist has to deal with at a crime scene. It makes up about 9 percent of a healthy person's body weight, and the average adult has about five to six liters of blood in his or her body. When blood is spilled, it goes a long way and is extremely difficult to remove completely. Murderers' attempts to clean up usually fail because blood tends to stick to clothing and the murder weapon, and is splashed around widely in a violent crime.

Blood found at crime scenes has trapped many killers who thought that they had removed all incriminating traces. Tests for blood are so sensitive that they will expose the presence of blood even after a surface has been wiped so that no blood is visible to the unaided eye. Blood that is many years old can still be identified as blood and analyzed for DNA.

Forensically, blood can yield a great deal of information. The first task for an investigator at a crime scene is to determine whether any suspicious stains are blood by doing a presumptive blood test. If the test is positive, then it must be determined if the blood is animal or human. Once this is established, the stains can be further tested for approximate age, sex, blood group, and now DNA.

Understanding how bloodstains and splashes appear under different circumstances can help enormously in reconstructing the sequence of events in a violent crime. Bloody fingerprints, palmprints, or footprints also tell their own stories and may be very helpful in solving the crime.

Composition of Blood

Blood is a very complex mixture. It consists of four main components: red blood cells, white blood cells, platelets, and plasma. Blood cells and platelets are all suspended in a pale yellow liquid called plasma.

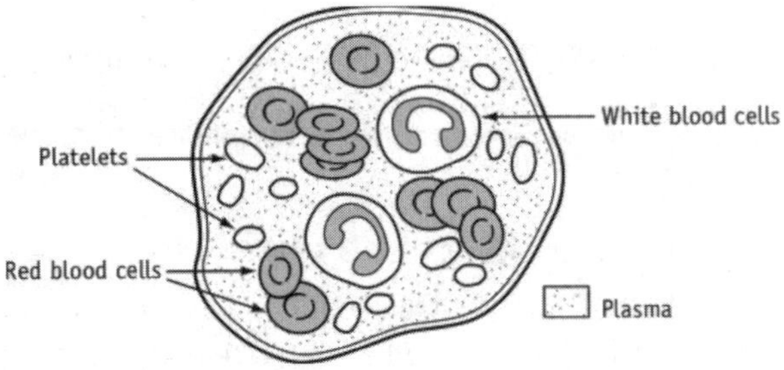

Red blood cells have a doughnut shape and give blood its color. They carry oxygen to the cells.

White blood cells are larger and less numerous than the red blood cells. They help destroy dangerous, foreign, or disease-causing organisms.

Platelets are tiny cell fragments that play an important role in blood clotting.

Plasma consists of 90 percent water and 10 percent dissolved proteins, hormones, salts, digested food materials, and waste products.

Comprehension Questions

1. How much blood does the average adult have in his or her body?
2. What information can blood found at a crime scene give investigators about the victim?
3. What other information can blood splashes give about how a crime was carried out?
4. In your science notebook, list the four main components of blood and give the main function of each component.

Blood Types

Before the 1900s, it was well known that if blood from one person came in contact with the blood of another person, very often the red blood cells would form clumps and would no longer be able to carry out their role.

In 1901, Austrian biologist Karl Landsteiner discovered that some people had certain antigens that could affect blood that did not have that antigen. The different blood types were named A (if it had only antigen A), B (if it had only antigen B), AB (if it had both A and B antigens), and O (if it had neither A nor B antigens). It was found that these blood types contain antibodies that react against the antigens, as shown in the table below.

Blood Group	Red Blood Cells Contain	Antibody in Plasma
A	A antigen	anti-B
B	B antigen	anti-A
AB	A and B antigens	no antibodies
O	no antigens	anti-A and anti-B

Every living person belongs to one of these four blood types. Which type is decided at the moment of conception and inherited from the parents. Hence, the blood type is fixed for life and does not change. This ABO system of blood typing interests forensic scientists because even if dried, the antigens can be detected and identified.

Today, the technique of DNA profiling can use blood to link a specific individual to a bloodstain. However, even before this development, a blood sample was considered important evidence if found at a crime scene.

Blood is a good example of a class characteristic, because it is associated with a group of people all having the same characteristic (that is, the same blood type). It is not unique to only one individual, like a fingerprint. Such evidence is still very important during investigations because it eliminates some suspects and so decreases the number of people who need to be examined.

This type of evidence allows the calculation of the probability that a sample of blood found at a crime scene came from a particular person. To do this, the proportion of the population belonging to that type or class needs to be known.

The table below shows the percentage of each blood type for some different populations.

	Blood Group (%)			
Population	A	B	AB	O
African American	28	20	5	47
Australian	39	11	4	46
Peruvian Indian	0	0	0	100
Polynesian	52	0	0	48
United Kingdom	41	10	4	45
United States	41	10	4	45

 © Shell Education

For example, if some B blood type was found at a crime scene in Australia, then all the people having a different type of blood (approximately 89 percent of the population) could be eliminated from further investigation. Hence, the probability that a particular person falls into the B group is 11 percent or approximately one in ten. The rarer the blood group the more useful the evidence.

Distribution of Blood Types

The previous table shows how some populations have a very different distribution of the four blood types. Distribution of type B blood is particularly interesting, because some population groups do not have this type at all, while in others it is quite rare, and yet it is quite common in other groups. The map below shows how the frequency of type B blood changes throughout the world. Some scientists believe that the changes in the distribution of the various blood types can be used as evidence to show the way in which ancient populations migrated around the world.

In forensic science, the frequency of the different blood types can be important. If a criminal in the United States shed some type O blood at a crime scene, it would rule out about 55 percent of the population as suspects but could not say which of the remaining 45 percent committed the crime. However, the most important aspect of blood typing has been to eliminate innocent suspects when their blood type has not matched the type that was left at a crime scene.

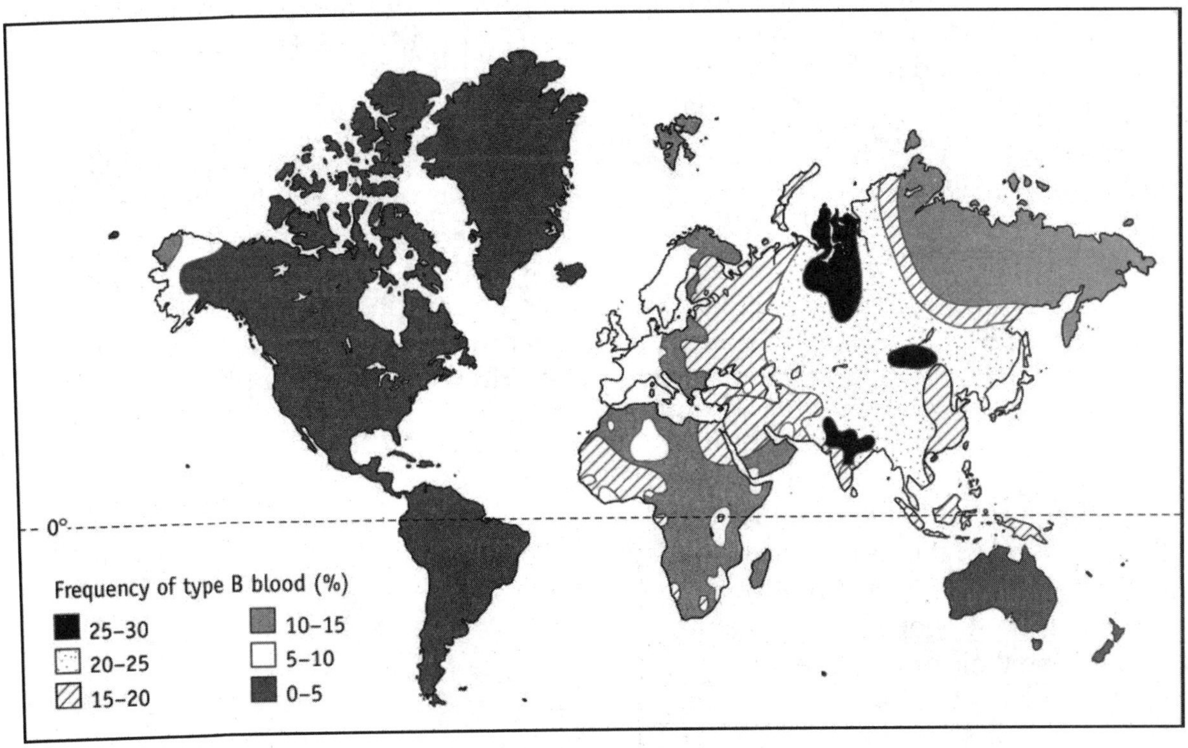

Blood (cont.)

Other Blood Types

In 1927, Dr. Landsteiner and his team discovered further blood typing factors that they named M & N. Later, in 1940, they discovered another very important antigen that reacted to the blood of the Indian rhesus monkey. This was named the Rh factor, and humans can be classified as either "Rh positive" if they have this antigen, or "Rh negative" if they do not. For example, in the United States, about 85% of the Caucasian population is Rh positive, about 94% of the African American and Hispanic populations are Rh positive, and about 98% of the Asian and Native American populations are Rh positive.

The Rh factor allows blood to be sorted into eight main types: A+, A–, B+, B–, O+, O–, AB+, AB–.

Further research has revealed a large number of proteins and enzymes that are found in plasma. Most are not stable once exposed to the air, but it is now possible to place an individual into one of 288 different blood typings, which can greatly increase the probability of linking a particular individual with a crime.

Secretors

Another discovery that has proven very important to the forensic biologist is that 80% of people are secretors. This means that a small number of blood cells are found in their other body fluids such as semen, urine, perspiration, and saliva. For these people, it is possible to determine their blood type by examining these fluids.

How Blood Types Are Inherited

A person's blood type is inherited from his or her parents. Look at the table below to see how blood types are passed on.

Parent 1	Parent 2	Possible	Impossible
O	O	O	A, B, AB
O	A	O, A	B, AB
O	B	O, B	A, AB
A	A	O, A	B, AB
A	B	AB, A, B, O	--
B	B	O, B	A, AB
O	AB	A, B	O, AB
A	AB	AB, A, B	O
B	AB	AB, A, B	O
AB	AB	AB, A, B	O

Research into hereditary factors in blood typing was often used for the purpose of establishing paternity. It cannot state with certainty that a child does come from specific parents, but it can determine whether a child is not the offspring of a given couple.

 © Shell Education

Human or Animal Blood?

The test used in the forensic laboratory to determine if blood is of human or animal origin is called the precipitin or Uhlenhuth Test, named after the German scientist who developed it. Blood of every animal species contains different proteins. Blood from one species will not accept proteins from another species. This principle is used to test whether bloodstains are human or animal, and if animal, which type.

Serum for the precipitin test is obtained from rabbits that have produced antibodies to destroy a small quantity of human blood injected into them. A drop of this antihuman serum is added to a sample of the suspect blood, which will precipitate its protein if the protein is of human origin. Most large forensic laboratories hold this antisera for many common animals, thus allowing the forensic biologist to confirm or disprove statements made by suspects about where they think certain dark brown stains may have come from.

This test is so sensitive that it has been successful in identifying human blood that is 15 years old and has even been used successfully on tissue samples from ancient Egyptian mummies.

Comprehension Questions

1. What discovery, made in 1901, meant that fewer people would die when they were given blood from someone else?
2. If some type A blood was found at a crime scene and one suspect had this same type of blood, what conclusions could you come to regarding the guilt of that suspect?
3. Which blood type of the four ABO types would be the most useful evidence to find at a crime scene? Explain why.
4. Where in the world do you think the B type blood may have originated? Describe how you think it may have spread across the world.
5. Explain what is meant by the term *secretor*. How can this help in solving a crime?
6. A murder victim has type AB blood. A suspect is found with a bloodstain of type AB on his shirt. Do you think this is enough evidence to prove the suspect's guilt? What would you think if the victim's blood type and the stain were both O+?
7. What do you think might happen to a person who has been transfused with blood containing an antibody different to his or her own blood antigen? Explain why this will occur.

Name ______________________________

Comparing Blood Samples

If a dark stain is found at a crime scene, it may be blood belonging to either the victim or criminal. Or it could be something else, like furniture polish or another dark stain. Before sending a sample to the lab for testing, the CSI must first establish that the stain is blood. For this reason, a presumptive blood test is done. This is a test that is quick and simple to carry out at the crime scene, confirming that the stain might be blood and so deserves further investigation.

There are two common ways such a test is done. In many countries, a KM (Kastle-Meyer) or LMG (leucomalachite green) test is done. In some states, forensic investigators use a hemastix. This is simply a plastic strip with a small square of special indicator paper attached to one end. Details of both procedures are described below.

Materials

- phenolphthalein (Kastle-Meyer or KM) solution
- leucomalachite green (LMG) solution
- hydrogen peroxide
- a number of small pieces of filter paper
- pipettes, if solutions are not in dropping bottles
- some dark brown or maroon stains, including dried animal blood and other substances, and also horseradish and fresh rust, each on a white ceramic tile

Procedure

1. Copy the results table below into your science notebook and use it to record observations.

Material	Observations for KM Solution	Observations for LMG Solution
blood stain		
horseradish		
fresh rust		

2. Fold one of the small filter papers into quarters as shown.

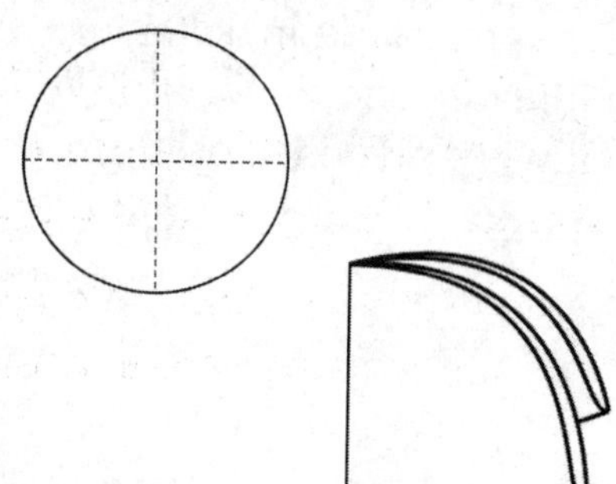

© Shell Education

Name ______________________

Comparing Blood Samples (cont.)

Procedure (cont.)

3. Scrape the dried stain with the sharp corner of the filter paper. Leave enough of each stain to repeat the test with the second solution if you have it available.
4. Open out the filter paper and add one drop of KM or LMG solution to the stain in the center.
5. Add one drop of hydrogen peroxide to the center. If there is blood present, you should see an instant color change.
6. Record your observations in the results table, and then repeat steps 2 to 5 using the second solution, and record these results as well.
7. Now repeat these presumptive blood tests using a small amount of horseradish, and then some fresh rust. Record these results as well.

Step 3

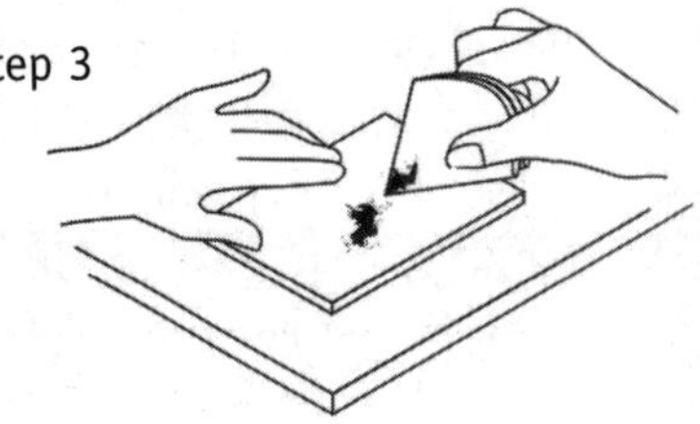

Step 4

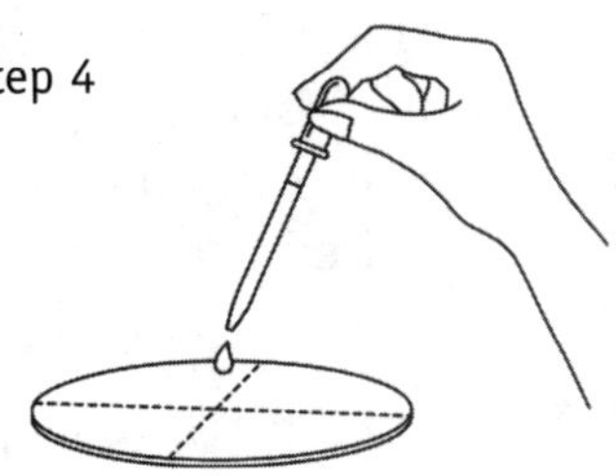

Step 5

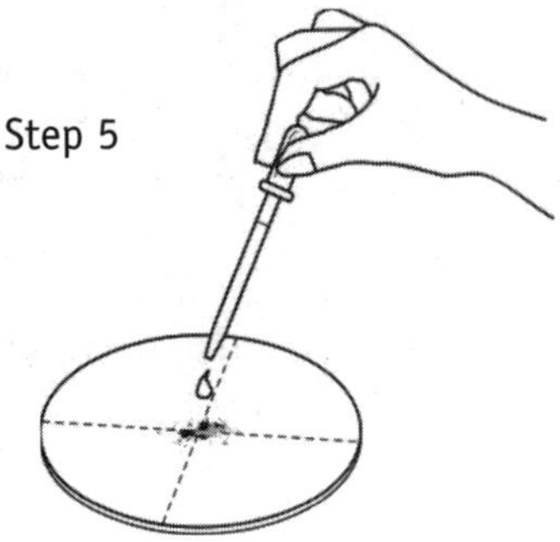

Analysis

1. What color did the blood turn the indicator?
2. What can you conclude regarding the accuracy of these tests to identify blood from the other dark red or brown stains?
3. Discuss how useful you think these tests are when used at a crime scene.
4. Make a list of all the steps a Crime Scene Investigator (CSI) would carry out if a suspicious dark brown stain were found at a crime scene in your local area.
5. If the stain showed positive to blood, what would you expect the CSI to do next?

Blood Splashes

Examination of blood splashes and smears at a crime scene is an essential part of a murder investigation. The position and appearance of blood marks on the body and surroundings will help the investigator to reconstruct the crime.

For example, because blood cannot flow uphill against gravity, it may indicate to the investigator that a body was moved after the victim was killed. The French criminologist Alexander Lacassagne is credited with linking the shape of blood spots with the position of the victim.

Blood dropped vertically onto a stationary, flat surface forms a circular mark with a serrated edge.

Drops of blood falling from a moving object hit a flat surface at an angle, leaving a spot like an exclamation mark, with a smaller spot showing the direction of movement. The arrow shows the way the person was moving.

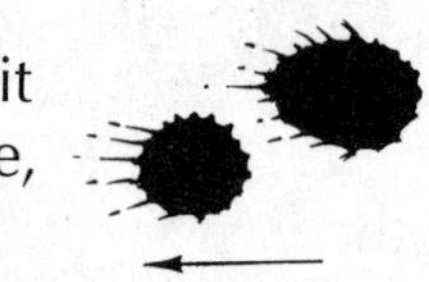

It is sometimes possible to make a rough estimate of the height from which blood fell by inspecting its edges. As the height increases, so does the length of the spines or serrations.

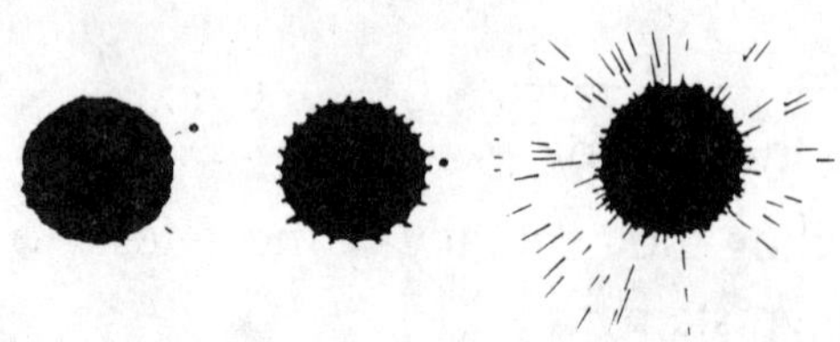

Examination of the shape of obliquely falling blood splashes yields information about the direction and speed of impact. Such evidence helps to determine the positions of the victim and assailant at the time of the assault and may indicate the degree of violence, the type of weapon used, and which person was the attacker and who was in a position of self-defense.

The shape of the blood splashes is approximately related to the steepness of the angle of fall. The thickness of the blood, due to the degree of clotting, also has some effect on the shape.

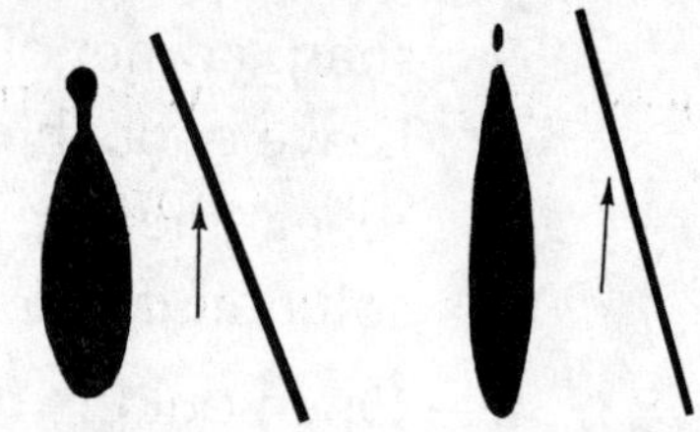

Blood smears tend to start as drops, which become ragged at one edge, indicating direction of travel of the smear. The arrow shows the direction in which the blood was smeared.

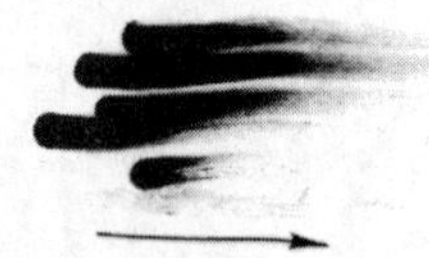

When a bloodied surface like hair is brushed against a clean surface a distinctive "swipe" pattern results.

If a clean surface moves against a bloodied one, a slightly different "wipe" pattern is produced. This commonly occurs when an attempt has been made to clean blood away.

Castoffs

When a bloodied weapon (hammer, axe, fist, etc.) is moved through the air, droplets of blood may be released behind the moving weapon and form a pattern. If the weapon should stop in midair, the droplets may be released and keep going in the same direction the weapon was moving before it was released. These droplets are known as *castoffs*.

© Shell Education

Blood Splashes (cont.)

Cast Offs (cont.)

Cast offs may give the following information:

- the direction the assailant's blow came from
- whether the assailant was right or left-handed
- how many swings were made
- how the weapon was swung
- how and where the assailant stood
- the position of the victim during the attack

Artery Damage and Blood Loss

An artery is a blood vessel that carries blood under great pressure from the heart to all the parts of the body. Hence, blood coming out of a damaged artery will spurt a long way, in big jets with each heartbeat, resulting in the loss of a lot of blood in a very short time.

Artery splashes are directly affected by the impact and so can be used to locate the origin of that impact.

Estimating the amount of blood lost can help determine the cause of death. If no body is found, it may determine that the victim must have died, or that a person having lost so much blood could not have defended himself or herself or caused the assault.

A large puddle of blood may identify the place where a body lay immediately after the crime while the blood still flowed.

Comprehension Questions

1. Describe four things that a CSI may be able to determine from the shape of some blood splashes at a crime scene.
2. Suggest how the splashes below may have occurred.

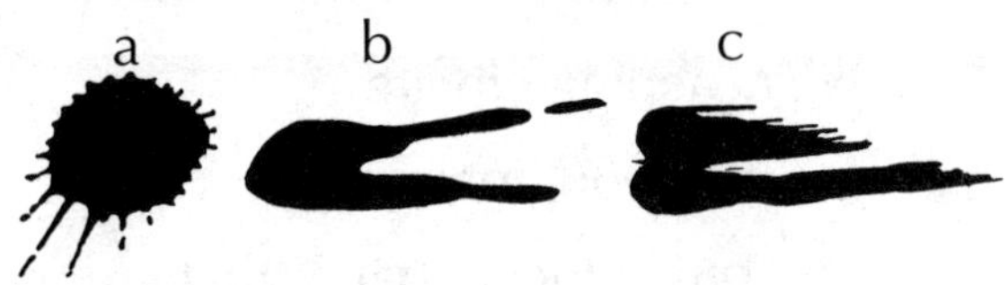

3. What is a cast off? Explain how they are formed and what information a Crime Scene Investigator may discover from these spots.
4. Discuss the effect on a victim if his or her major artery is damaged during a violent attack, and describe what an investigator might find afterward at such a crime scene.
5. Describe the steps a junior police officer should follow if suddenly called to a violent crime scene where there is a lot of blood splashed around, and one person is found sobbing over what appears to be a body. Explain the reason for each step that you suggest.

Name ______________________

Blood Splashes

In this activity you are going to investigate how the shape and pattern of blood splashes change under different circumstances, and then apply this knowledge to cases of criminal investigations.

Materials

- red (water soluble) dye that has been thickened with gelatin
- newspaper and some butcher paper for the tests
- meter ruler
- dropping pipette
- plywood board
- some other surfaces that are more porous than the paper (such as cloth) and some less porous (such as ceramic tile)

Note: Paint may be given a more bloodlike consistency by dissolving gelatin in it.

Procedure

1. Copy the tables below into your science notebook under the heading "Results."

Height	Diameter of Solid Center	Other Observations
10 cm		
30 cm		
60 cm		
1 m		
2 m		

Tilt and Height	Diameter of Center	Length of Splashes	Shape of Splashes
30° at 20 cm			
30° at 80 cm			
70° at 20 cm			
70° at 80 cm			

Walking Speed	Distance between Splashes	Shape and Size of Splashes
slow		
fast		

 © Shell Education

Name ______________________________

Blood Splashes (cont.)

Procedure (cont.)

2. Cover the floor thoroughly with newspaper and then place some butcher paper over the center where the "blood" splashes are going to be dropped.
3. Using a ruler, measure a height of 10 cm above the butcher paper, and then drop one drop of dye from this height. Label the drop "10 cm," then drop the following drop next to the first drop from 30 cm.
4. Repeat this procedure dropping more dye from 60 cm, 1 m, and 2 m, or other heights your group chooses to test.
5. Sketch some of the drops in your science notebooks, carefully labeling each with the height. Compare their shapes and fill in the first table.
6. Now take a board and cover it with butcher paper, then tilt it about 30° from the floor.
7. Drip red dye onto the paper from two different heights (for example, 20 cm and 80 cm). Record your results in the second table.
8. Repeat step 7 with the board tilted at 70° from the floor. Try other angles such as 80° or 90° if you have time.
9. Lay some butcher paper along the floor and slowly walk along the paper, dropping a drop of dye each time your left foot touches the floor. Measure the distances between the splashes and observe their shapes.
10. Repeat step 9, but this time walk quickly.
11. Repeat steps 1–10, dropping dye splashes onto materials that have different surfaces, and compare their appearances.

Analysis

1. What change occurred in the appearance of the blood splashes as the height increased? Sketch three spots to show how their shapes changed.
2. Use a diagram to show how the shape changes when blood falls onto a sloping surface, and describe how the angle of the slope affects the shape.

Name ____________________

Blood Splashes (cont.)

Analysis (cont.)

3. What was the effect of movement on the shape of the spots? Did speed affect their shape? What did you notice about the distance between the spots when the speed was faster? Why would such knowledge be of help to a crime scene investigator?
4. Describe how the thickness of blood can affect the shape of the blood spots. Suggest a way in which you could test your hypothesis.
5. Under what circumstances could blood be thicker than what you would normally expect to flow from a wound?
6. Discuss how knowledge of all these influences on the pattern and shape of blood splashes can contribute to help an investigator solve a crime.

 © Shell Education

DNA

DNA is short for *deoxyribonucleic acid.* DNA is a gigantic molecule found in the nucleus of every cell and in every living organism. It looks something like a ladder with about 3 billion rungs, and is the chemical of which chromosomes are made. Chromosomes are large entwined strands of DNA. They can be divided into smaller sections called *alleles*, which encode instructions for cell operation. These instructions are *genes*, and they are passed down from parent to child through alleles in DNA. The DNA from related people is always more similar than DNA from unrelated people. In the same way, the DNA of closely related animals and plants is also more alike than the DNA of organisms that are only distantly related. It has been found that human DNA has about 90% of its alleles in common with the DNA of other primates.

The only people who share exactly the same DNA are identical twins, because they started out as a single fertilized egg. In its early stages, this egg split apart and then grew into two separate babies who are genetically identical.

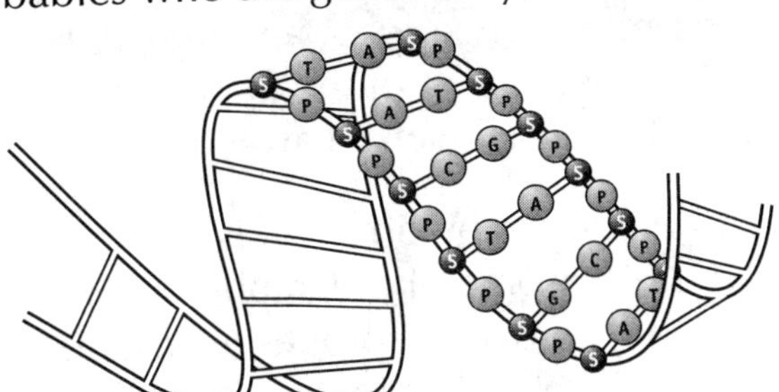

The legs of the "ladder" consist of alternating molecules called *sugars and phosphates* (marked as "s" and "p" in the diagram above). The ladder twists itself into a "double helix" to save room as it fits into the nucleus. The rungs of the DNA ladder are made up of pairs of molecules called bases. There are only four different bases, and they always pair up in exactly the same way. Adenine (A) always pairs with thymine (T), and cytosine (C) always attaches to guanine (G).

The DNA ladder has also been compared to a zipper with the four bases forming the teeth. The difference is that in order to join the two strands of DNA, A must pair with T, and G must pair with C. The order in which these bases appear is the genetic code that determines all inherited characteristics.

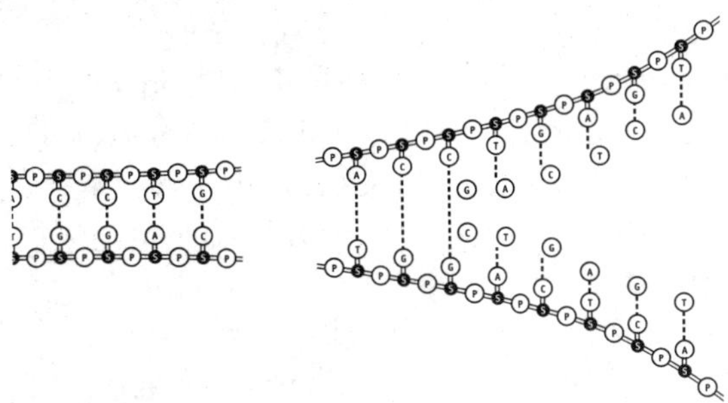

This DNA, or genetic code, is unique to every person and is a combination of which 50% is inherited from the father and 50% from the mother. When a cell divides in two, it opens like a zipper, and the DNA copies this order of bases exactly, so the DNA in the new cell is identical to the DNA in the original cell.

Comprehension Questions

1. Where in our bodies is DNA found? Explain the purpose of this molecule.
2. Describe how DNA is able to make an exact copy of itself when a cell splits into two new cells.
3. DNA is not as unique to all individuals as fingerprints are. Explain the difference, and discuss which type of evidence you think is better and why.

DNA (cont.)

Comprehension Questions (cont.)

4. What is meant by the term *genetic code*? Explain how this chemical DNA is able to instruct the body to produce red hair, blue eyes, or a certain nose shape.

DNA Profiling

DNA profiling is probably the most important discovery for use in forensic science since the development of fingerprinting over a hundred years ago. While blood typing can positively exclude a suspect, it can only give a probability as to guilt. DNA profiling can actually prove a person's identity, except in the case of identical twins. No wonder it has been said to have revolutionized crime solving.

Professor Alec Jeffreys

It was in September of 1984 at Leicester University, England, that Professor Alec Jeffreys stumbled across his exciting discovery. He was working on parts of DNA where there was a sequence of bases that varied greatly in unrelated individuals. He and his team found a way in which these sequences could be made visible as X-ray lines that looked a little like a bar code. These "bar codes" give a unique pattern for every person, hence the original term of *genetic fingerprinting*.

Producing a DNA Profile

1. A blood or hair sample is collected from a suspect and a garment found at a crime scene.
2. The DNA is extracted in the laboratory, then "cut" into small pieces using a scissorslike chemical called an enzyme. The lengths of these fragments differ greatly from person to person.
3. Next, these pieces are placed in a gel through which an electric current is passed. The current carries the fragments along through the gel. The shorter pieces move faster, so they end up farther along than the longer pieces.
4. A chemical is added that causes the two strands of DNA to unlink like a zipper being opened. The sorted DNA fragments are now transferred to a sheet of nylon.
5. Radioactive strands of DNA (called probes) are added, and they link up with some of the fragments. The rest are rinsed away.
6. When the nylon sheet is placed under some photographic film, the radioactive probes expose it, and when developed, they leave a pattern that resembles a bar code.
7. This pattern of dark bands from the suspect's blood is compared to the pattern made by the DNA from the crime scene. If they match, the two samples are from the same person.

© Shell Education

Producing a DNA Profile *(cont.)*

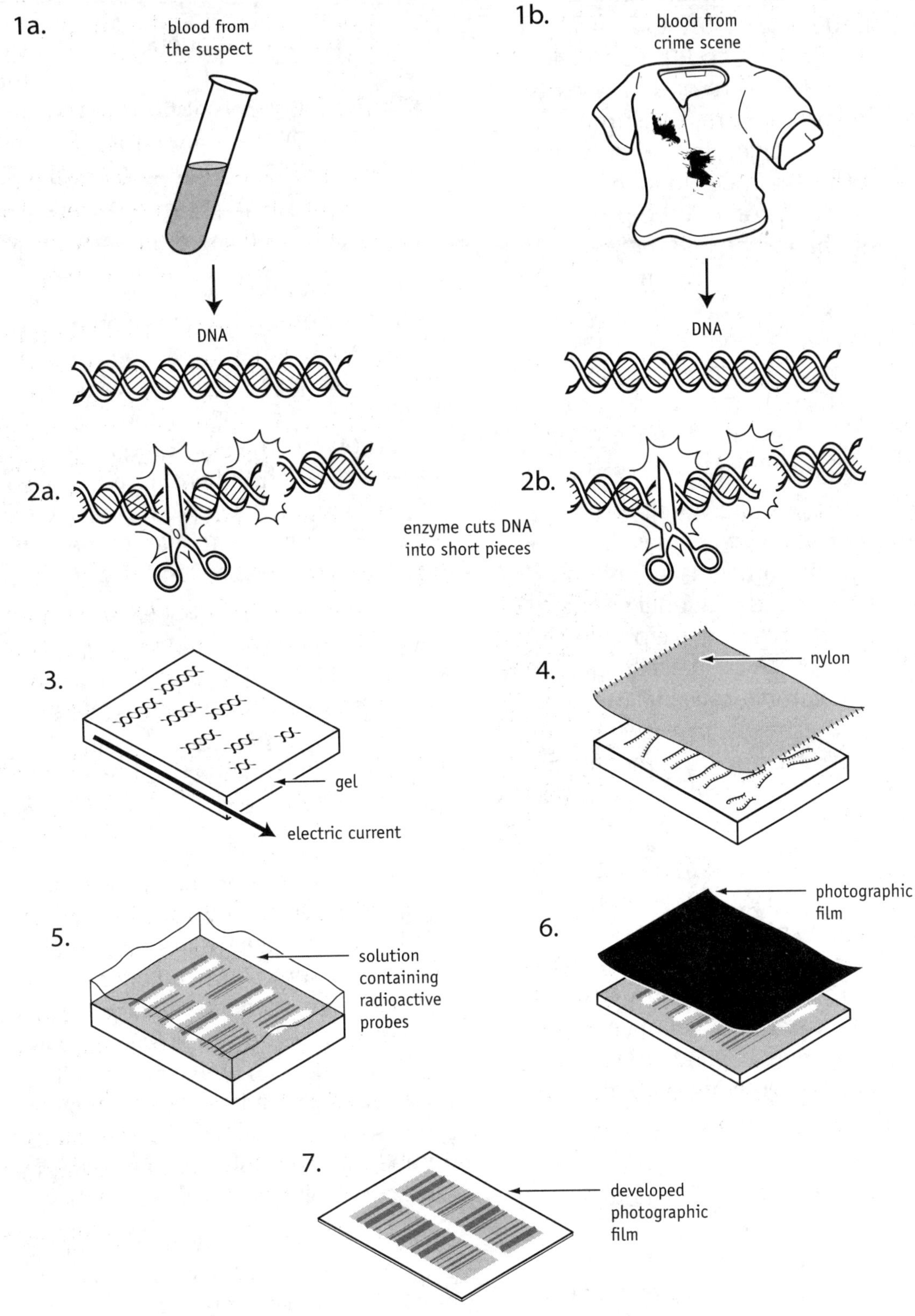

DNA (cont.)

Modern Developments in DNA Profiling

Although the original method was very discriminating and the odds of a random match were one in several billion, it was very timeconsuming and therefore expensive. In the early days of DNA analysis, it could take up to six weeks for a profile to be produced. Also, there had to be a sufficient quantity of the biological material and it had to be in good condition. Unfortunately, in forensic situations this is often not the case, because DNA is easily damaged by heat or bacteria. Very often, evidence cannot be collected while it is still fresh.

Modern techniques now include an amplification (copying) process in which very small amounts of DNA are duplicated over and over until enough has been made to produce a profile. In fact, sufficient DNA can be extracted from only a few hair roots, saliva left on a drink bottle, licked stamp, or in chewing gum that has been chewed in the mouth. Even skin cells left on clothes that have rubbed against the body may be used.

The downside of this extreme sensitivity is that it is much easier for a sample of biological material to become contaminated with DNA from the person collecting it, or any other innocent person who has come in contact with the crime scene. Hence, great care must be taken by anyone entering such an area or carrying out the analysis.

The parts of DNA that are chosen for analysis are small sections where, for some unknown reason, a group of bases repeat themselves, like a stutter. These parts do not appear to have anything to do with our inherited characteristics. It is these sections of DNA that are being amplified and analyzed to give a person's profile.

For example, if a sequence of bases is saying G C T T A C T G T G A T C, the bases appear to occur completely at random. However, a couple of bases may unexpectantly repeat like this:

G C T T A C T A C T A C T A C T A C T G T G A T C

It has been found that the number of repeats varies for different people. So Person A might have five repeats as shown above, but Person B might have only four repeats, while Person C might have 12 repeats of the same short sequence. Now, if several of such stutter sites are looked at, the chance of two people having exactly the same number of repeats of the same sections becomes very unlikely.

Most developed countries now use a system called Second Generation Multiplex (SGM) that copies 10 such sections of the DNA as well as incorporating a sex marker. Using these 11 parts, the technique is extremely sensitive and has a discrimination order of 1 in 1,000 million.

Many jurisdictions maintain databases of DNA profiles. They contain records of all profiles collected from unsolved crimes and from convicted offenders. Samples from offenders are taken either from blood, mouth swabs (buccal cells), or head hair. Each time a new profile is added, it is searched against all other profiles already in the database. A large number of previously unsolved crimes have been solved using these databases.

Analysis now takes only 48 hours and is getting quicker. The cost has also come down so that the technique is being used

© Shell Education

DNA (cont.)

routinely for nonserious crimes like house burglaries and car theft. DNA profiling is now helping to solve many crimes that were not able to be solved previously.

Matching DNA Profiles

DNA profiling, as well as being extremely important in trapping killers and rapists, is also used routinely to establish the identity of a child's father in paternity disputes or in proving family links in immigration applications.

A child inherits half of his or her chromosomes, and hence DNA, from each parent. In cases of disputed paternity, DNA profiles are obtained from the mother, the child, and both men claiming to be the father. Each band on the child's profile must match one on either the mother's or father's profile as shown here. Hence, it is possible to identify the real father.

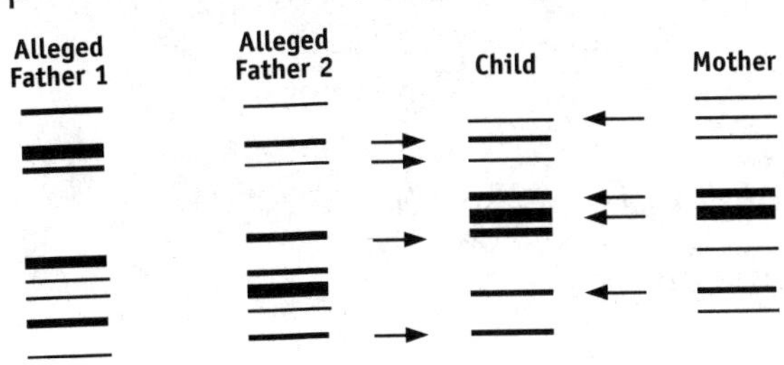

The child's real father above is father 2, whose profile has about half the bars in common with the child. The other bars on the child's profile come from the mother.

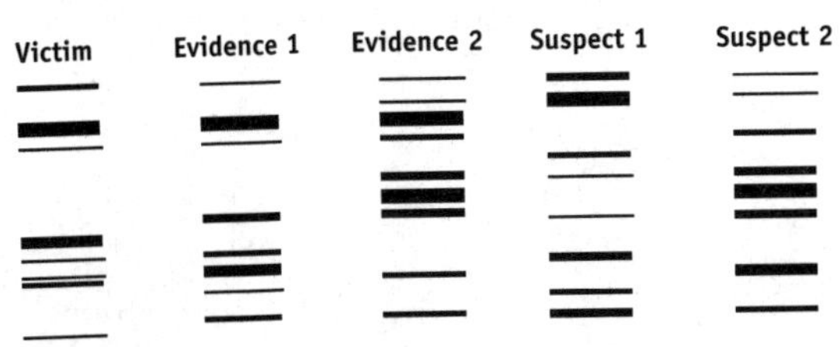

In the diagram above, the DNA profiles from the victim and that found at the crime scene (Evidence 1 and 2) closely match the profile from Suspect 2, hence implicating him. Suspect 1's profile has no bars in common with the evidence, so he is most likely innocent of the crime.

Comprehension Questions

1. Who is credited with the discovery of DNA profiling? When and where was this discovery made?
2. Discuss three disadvantages of the original profiling technique for use in forensic science.
3. Describe modern developments that have been made to overcome these problems.
4. How has the time taken to produce a DNA profile changed since it was first developed?
5. Describe what is stored in forensic DNA databases, and describe how it is used to solve crimes.
6. Describe some other uses of DNA profiling aside from its use in forensic science.
7. Explain how blood found on some window glass at a crime scene can be used to discover who broke the window and climbed in to burgle the house.
8. List the evidence from which DNA may be collected and try to put it in order of what you think may be the most useful to a forensic scientist to the least useful. Explain your answer.

Name ______________________

Extracting DNA

DNA can be extracted from a number of organisms by the following steps:

1. breaking down the cell and nuclear membranes (called "lysing" the cells with a detergent)
2. breaking down and removing cellular proteins by dissolving them
3. precipitating out the DNA (done with ethanol)

Dried chickpeas are rich in DNA as well as proteins and starch, so the latter are the components that are removed in this activity. A typical pea cell can be represented by the following diagram.

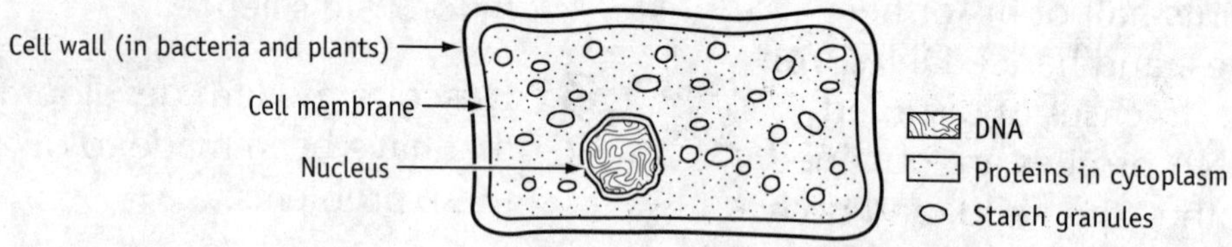

Note: Solution A is a buffering and salt solution, Solution B is a membrane lysing solution, Solution C is a buffering, lysing and salt-stabilizing solution, and Solution D is a nuclear membrane lysing solution. The "soup" is made before the lesson. See notes at the end of page 56 for details.

Materials

- solution A (10 mM MgCl2, 10 mM Tris buffer pH 7.5 and 0.2 M NaCl)
- solution B (Triton X-100, 20% in distilled water)
- 1 g dried chickpeas
- centrifuge
- solution C (0.5% Triton X-100, and 10 mM Tris, 10 mM MgCl2 pH 7.5)
- 2 plastic centrifuge test tubes
- solution D (1% SDS in distilled water)
- 1 small glass test tube
- ice cold ethanol
- 3 plastic pipettes
- cotton gauze
- glass rod with hook at one end

 © Shell Education

Name ______________________

Extracting DNA (cont.)

Procedure

1. Make "pea soup" by grinding chickpeas with 10 mL solution A, then stirring for one hour with 0.25 mL solution B.

2. Filter 10 mL of the "pea soup" through gauze into your first plastic test tube.

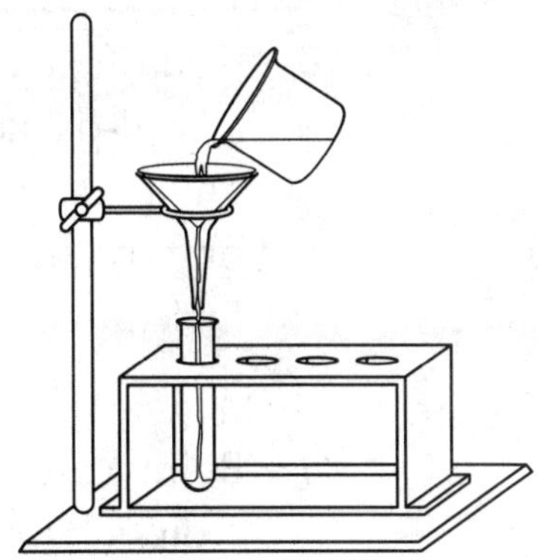

Step 2

3. Centrifuge at 3000 rpm until a well-packed pellet is formed. The liquid above the solid pellet contains the unwanted proteins and salts.

4. Pour off this liquid (which is called the supernatant) and keep the pellet, which consists of starch and cell nuclei containing DNA.

Step 3

5. Add 10 mL of solution C to the pellet left in the test tube. Stir gently with the pipette until the pellet is completely broken up.

6. Centrifuge again at 3500 rpm for 4 minutes until another well-packed pellet is formed, and again discard the liquid at the top, which contains more protein.

7. Add 4 mL of solution D and stir gently with the pipette until all lumps are removed.

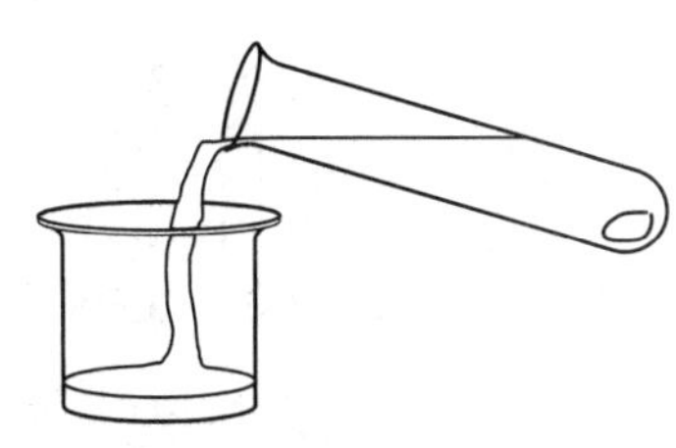

Step 4

Name ____________________

Extracting DNA (cont.)

Procedure (cont.)

8. Centrifuge once more at 3000 rpm to form a well-packed pellet. KEEP THE LIQUID. The pellet is mainly starch, but the liquid on top (the supernatant) will contain your DNA.

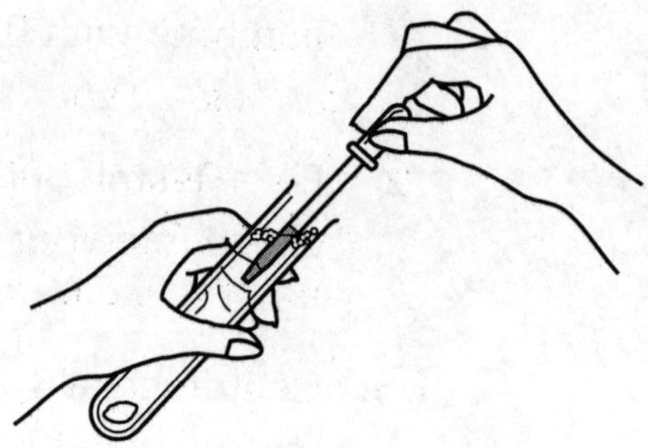

Step 9

9. Being careful not to disturb the pellet, use a pipette to extract about 2 mL from the middle of the supernatant and transfer it into a clean glass test tube. Leave behind the foam on top of the liquid.

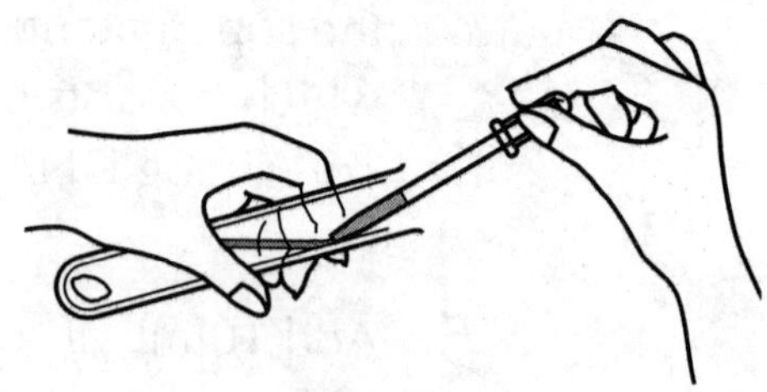

Step 10

10. Tilt the glass test tube and, using a clean pipette, slowly add 3 mL of icy cold ethanol down the side so that it forms a layer on top of the DNA solution rather than mixing with it.

11. Now use the glass hook to gently stir the layer where the ethanol touches the DNA solution and observe the formation of the long strands of DNA. If you can scoop the DNA onto the end of the glass rod, you should be able to lift it out of the test tube.

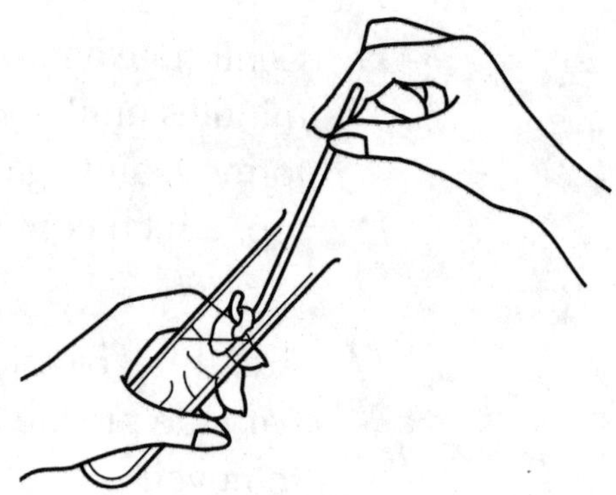

Step 11

Note: DNA is fairly transparent. If your DNA appears whitish, it is from contamination with protein that was not completely removed in the earlier steps.

Steps 2 to 6 are to remove protein, and steps 7 to 9 are to remove the DNA from the starch.

© Shell Education

Name ______________________________

Extracting DNA (cont.)

Analysis

1. Write out a description of the method that you used to extract your DNA.
2. Under the heading "Results," describe the appearance and quantity of your final product. Compare your product with other groups and describe how successful your group was at extracting DNA from dried peas.
3. If the quantity or quality of DNA that your group extracted was less than others, discuss some reasons why this might have been. Suggest where you might make improvements if you had time to repeat this activity.

Paint Chips

Small fragments of paint can be chipped off when a hard object strikes a painted surface. For example, this may occur when a car strikes something or someone. If a thief tries to pry open a window, the tool may remove some flakes of paint. These flakes can be unique if the building is an older one that has been repainted several times.

If such paint chips are found, they can be placed vertically (held up by modeling clay or putty) under a stereoscopic microscope, and the different layers of paint can be examined. It is not unusual for some older cars to have up to 10 layers of paint, including binding materials. In each case, the colors and the order of these colors are unique for different makes and models of cars. The scientist is able to examine the layers in the flakes for color, texture, sequence, and thickness.

These days, the color layers for all models of cars are supplied by the car manufacturer and are recorded on a computer database. This allows the forensic scientist to quickly discover the color, make, model, and year of manufacture of the car from a paint chip.

If the paint chips found at a crime scene match the paint on a suspect's car, then that car was probably at the scene. Often, dents or damage are further evidence that incriminates the suspect.

Some paints and binders used on the car body can be dissolved in some solvents such as acetone (found in nail polish remover) or butane (cigarette lighter fuel). Paint chips can be placed in a number of different solvents and examined to see if there is any seepage of color from any of the layers. If the same layer in two different chips dissolves in the same solvent, and the order of the other layers is the same, it can be concluded that the two chips are probably from the same object.

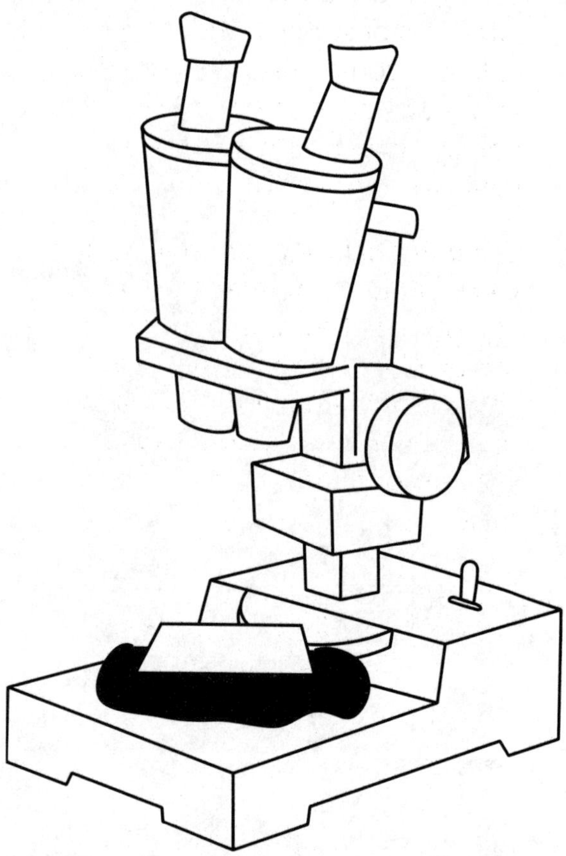

© Shell Education

Paint Chips (cont.)

Comprehension Questions

1. Describe two tests that can be carried out to determine if two paint chips are from the same source.
2. If the layers of paint, fillers, and binders of a paint flake taken from a crime scene exactly match the order and thickness of the layers in another paint flake from a suspect's car, what conclusion can an investigator make regarding the suspect?
3. What other information would be needed before an arrest should be made?
4. If two paint flakes both had the same eight layers of the same colors, in the same order, but the thickness of some of the layers differed, could you conclude that they probably came from the same object? Explain the reasons for your answer.
5. The paint flakes (a) to (d) at right were found at the crime scene. The paint flakes A to D were removed from four suspect cars. Do any of the paint flakes match up? Which ones, if any? What conclusions can you draw from this?

a

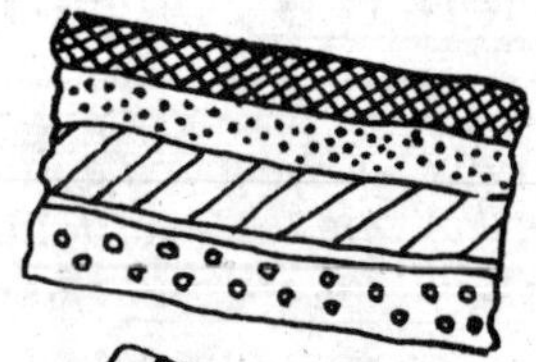

b

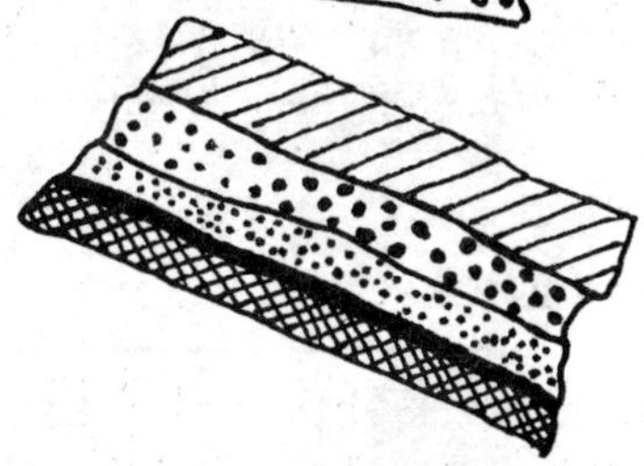

c

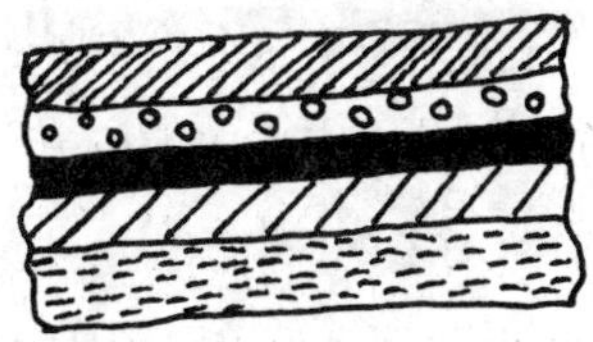

d

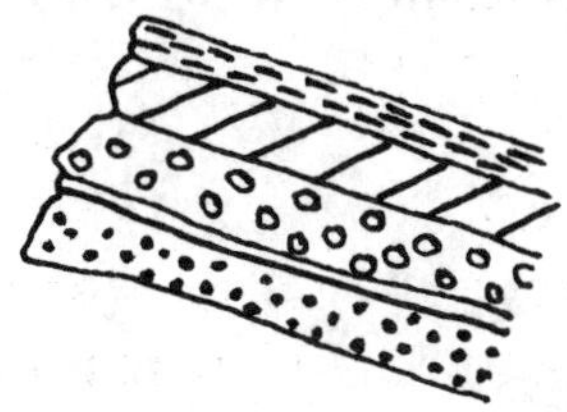

A

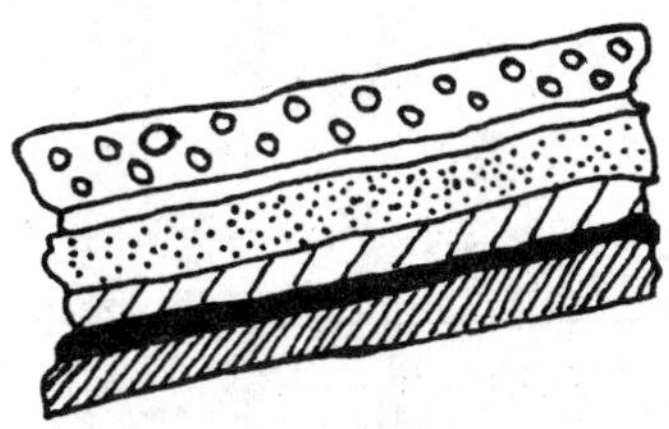

B

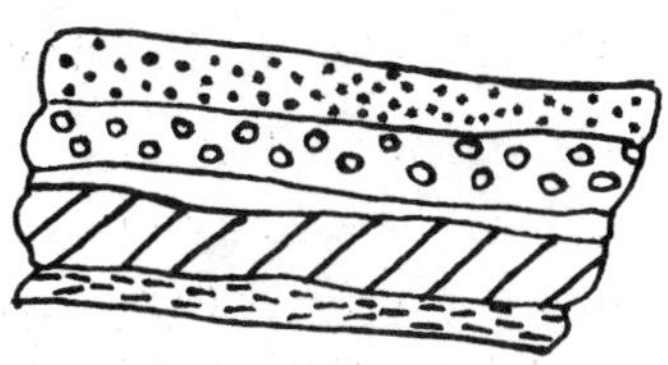

C

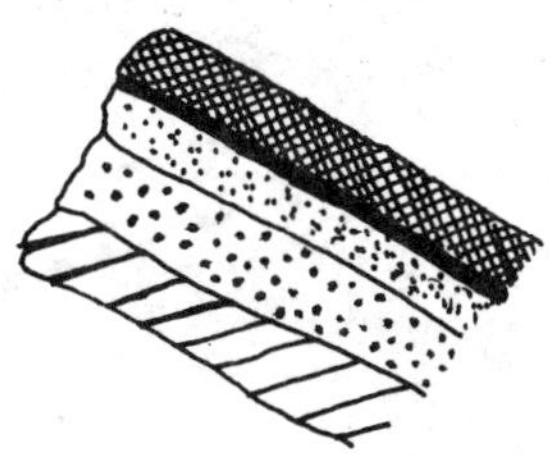

D

Name ______________________

Comparing Paint Flakes

In this activity you will be given a number of paint flakes collected from several damaged suspect vehicles, as well as one that was found embedded in the wooden gatepost at the site of a house burglary. The CSI thinks that the gate may have been hit by the getaway car.

Your task is to see if the chip from the crime scene matches any of the suspect cars by examining the paint layers and testing the solubility of the different layers.

Materials

- a number of paint flakes labeled to indicate their source
- a microscope (preferably stereoscope, but a compound one will do)
- small amount of modeling clay
- microscope slide
- ceramic tile with indentations
- acetone
- ethanol
- butane

Note: Acetone, butane, and ethanol are all flammable, so only a small amount should be used in the little indentations in the tile, and they should be kept away from flames.

Procedure

1. Place the paint chip vertically in the modeling clay on the slide.

 © Shell Education

Name ______________________________

Comparing Paint Flakes (cont.)

Procedure (cont.)

2. Adjust the microscope to low power and examine the paint chip layers.

Inspecting a paint chip edge through a microscope

3. Record the number of layers of paint, their colors, and thicknesses in a table in your science notebook.
4. Place a small part of the paint chip in three of the indentations on the ceramic tile. Add a drop of acetone to one chip, ethanol to the next one, and butane to the last one. Look for any sign of color bleeding or dissolving.
5. Repeat for all the paint chips and record your results.

Analysis

1. Draw a table in your science notebook showing how all the flakes compared in each of the tests.
2. Was one of the suspect chips identical to the one found at the crime scene? If so, which one?
3. List all the similarities between the two.
4. Would this evidence be enough to incriminate the driver of this car? Discuss the reasons for your answer.
5. What other information would be useful to the police investigating this crime?

Infrared and Ultraviolet Light

When sunlight passes through a prism, it separates into a whole series of different colors that we call the *visible spectrum*. These are the same as the colors of a rainbow. This was discovered by Sir Isaac Newton in 1666. Each color is associated with a different wavelength.

The visible spectrum is only a small part of the electromagnetic spectrum. On both sides of these visible colors are other rays that are not visible. The region beyond the red color, with wavelengths longer than 10^{-6} m, is the infrared region (see graph below). Infrared radiation is used in heat lamps and high-speed ovens. Waves that have even longer wavelengths than the infrared rays include microwaves and radio and television waves.

The region beyond the violet color, with wavelengths less than 10^{-7} m, is the ultraviolet region. These rays have a lot of energy and can cause significant damage to your eyes if you look at them. There are ultraviolet rays in sunlight, and they tan the skin; however, too many can cause sunburn. Rays with even shorter wavelengths than ultraviolet light include X-rays and gamma rays used in medicine.

The forensic scientist uses both the infrared (IR) and ultraviolet (UV) parts of the spectrum as well as visible light. The ultraviolet light causes some substances to fluoresce, or glow. We say such substances or materials are fluorescent. Some objects continue to glow after the light has been removed. We say these things are *phosphorescent*.

Substances like some washing powders contain small amounts of fluorescent chemicals so that they glow bluish-white in sunlight, giving the impression of whiteness. Some oils also fluoresce under UV light, so oils that may appear the same under normal sunlight can look quite different under UV light.

Other contact traces that forensic scientists may examine and compare under UV light include fabrics and fibers, paint samples, inks and dyes, and even glass fragments.

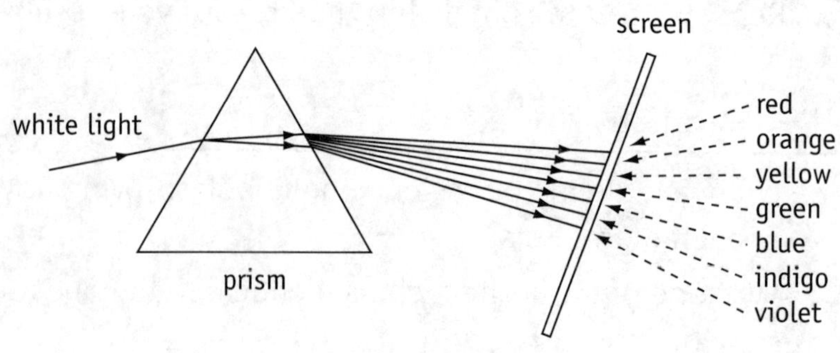

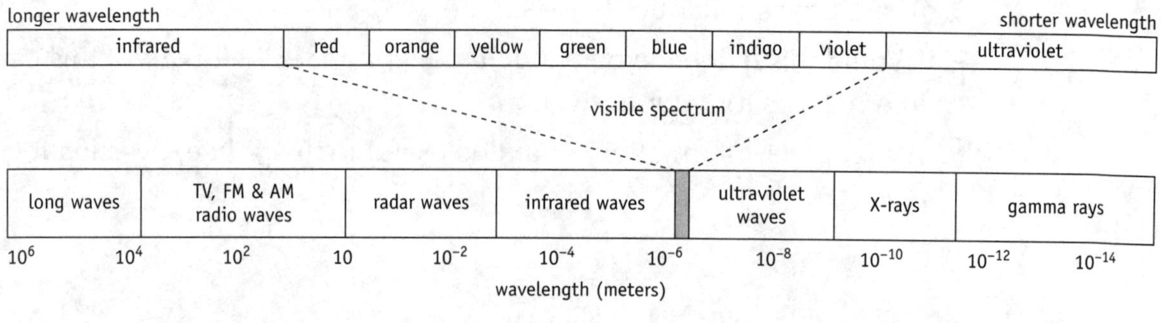

© Shell Education

Infrared and Ultraviolet Light (cont.)

Comprehension Questions

1. Explain what the visible spectrum is, and how it can be displayed.
2. What are the colors of the visible spectrum, in order from longest to shortest wavelength?
3. Describe how ultraviolet and infrared are different from visible light.
4. Explain how ultraviolet radiation can be used in the forensic laboratory to help solve a crime.
5. What is the difference between fluorescent and phosphorescent?

Name ______________________

Liquids in UV Light

In this activity you will examine a collection of oils, such as mechanical, baby, cooking, paraffin, and sewing-machine oils. Other liquids that could be inspected include gasoline samples, tonic water, washing detergent, and other household substances. These should be examined under natural and UV light.

Note: Take care to never look directly at a UV lamp. Also be careful not to have an exposed flame near flammable liquids such as oil and gasoline.

Materials

- selection of different oils and similar liquids
- some absorbent paper such as filter paper
- UV lamp

Procedure

1. Copy the following table in your science notebook, under the heading "Examining Oils and Other Liquids Under UV Light."

Type of Oil or Liquid	Appearance in Natural Light	Appearance in UV Light

2. Place a few drops of each of the liquids on the absorbent paper or inspect each liquid in its clear container.
3. Examine each substance, first in natural light, then under the UV light.
4. Record the appearance of each substance under each light in your table.

Analysis

1. Which substances showed the greatest change in appearance when viewed under UV light?
2. List all the substances that showed a moderate change in appearance.
3. Which substances were nonfluorescent?
4. Describe a possible crime in which a forensic scientist may examine evidence under UV light.

© Shell Education

Spectroscopes

A simple, small instrument called a spectroscope can be used by scientists to produce a very clear spectrum. German scientists Robert Kirchoff and Robert Bunsen first developed it in the 1850s. It consists of a long brass tube with a prism at one end.

Looking at a colored flame through a spectroscope

These scientists found that if some elements were heated, they began to glow and produce light of their own characteristic color. If they allowed the light to pass through the spectroscope, the light separated into a series of distinct bright lines of various colors.

The normal visible spectrum is a continuous spectrum, where one color merges into the next. It can be seen if the spectroscope is held up to normal light. The spectrum produced by heating different chemicals is called a line spectrum, because it is a series of brightly colored lines, separated by dark bands. Each element produces its own unique pattern of bright lines. If the spectroscope is used to view the colored light produced when a salt is heated in a flame, these colored bands can be seen, as shown below for sodium, potassium, and calcium.

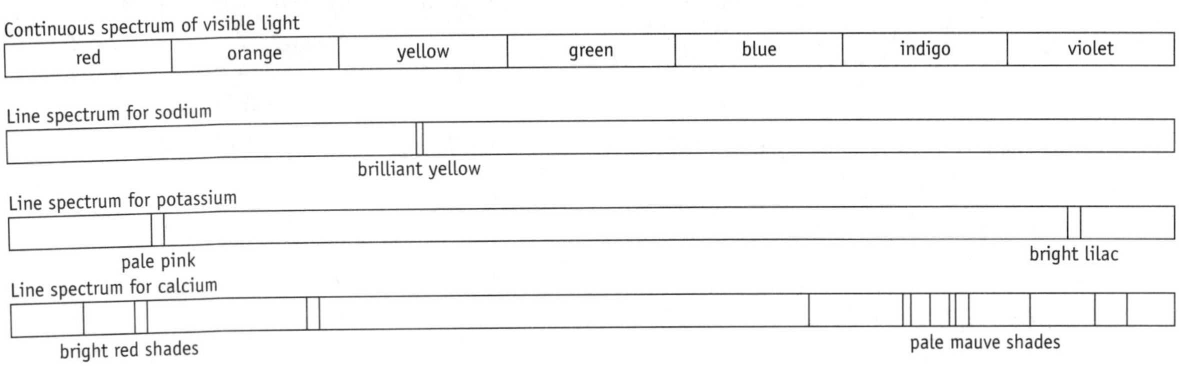

Spectroscopes (cont.)

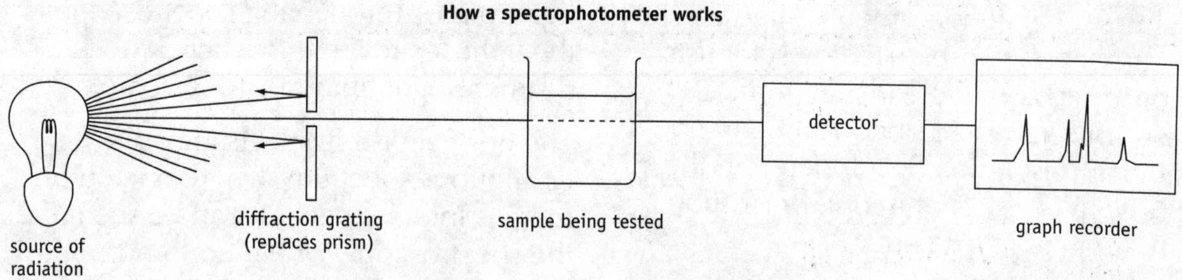

In the forensic laboratory, scientists use more sophisticated instruments such as the spectrophotometer, which is based on the same principle as the spectroscope, but can actually measure the intensity of each wavelength in the sample, and can identify the proportion of each element in a substance. This is very useful when comparing two substances that appear very similar and have to be chemically analyzed.

The advantage of this technique is that only small amounts of the substances are needed, but the disadvantage is that the substance must be destroyed in order to find what chemicals are in it.

Comprehension Questions

1. Color in the colors of the continuous spectrum in the illustration on page 65, fading one color into the next. Use colored lines to color in the line spectra of the three metal elements.
2. Explain what a spectroscope is, and what it can be used for.
3. Describe how the line spectrum of sodium is different from a line spectrum of potassium.
4. Why would a forensic scientist prefer to use a spectrophotometer rather than a spectroscope?
5. Explain under what circumstances a forensic scientist may need to identify an unknown substance.
6. What is one advantage of using the spectrophotometer in forensic science, and what is one disadvantage of this technique?

© Shell Education

Name ____________________

Spectroscopy

In this activity you will investigate the flame color of a number of metal compounds, including several containing the same metal ion component and several having the same nonmetal ion component.

Materials

- labeled vials containing some different metal compounds (salts)
- two vials of unknown salts
- Bunsen burner
- spectroscope
- platinum wire (one per compound)

Note: Because it is difficult to remove the compounds from the platinum wire, it is recommended that one wire remain with each salt throughout the experiment, and that the students move around the room, testing each compound at its own location. Cleaning can then be done without students handling concentrated hydrochloric acid.

Procedure

1. Create the following table in your science notebook under the heading "Looking at Flame Colors."

Type of Salt	Flame Color	Additional Observations

2. Light the Bunsen burner.
3. Wet the wire with a little water, then dip it into the salt. Hold the wire in the flame and look for the first color to appear. Repeat if unsure.
4. Repeat step three with all the other salts. Then use the information from the named salts tested to identify parts of the compound in the two unknown samples.

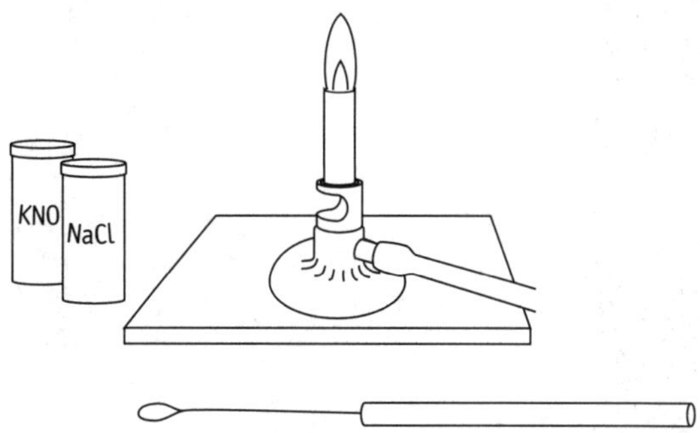

Name ____________________

Spectroscopy (cont.)

Analysis

1. Many compounds have different flame colors. Do you think the distinctive color is from the metal or nonmetal ions of the compound? Explain what has led you to this conclusion.
2. Was it possible to identify the other ion of the compound? Explain your answer.
3. Suggest a situation in which a forensic scientist could use flame colors to help solve a crime.
4. Using chemistry textbooks from the library, find out what a salt and an ion are, and what causes the distinctive flame color in some salts. Make a list of as many different metals as you can, each with its own unique color.
5. Why was the wire made wet in step three?

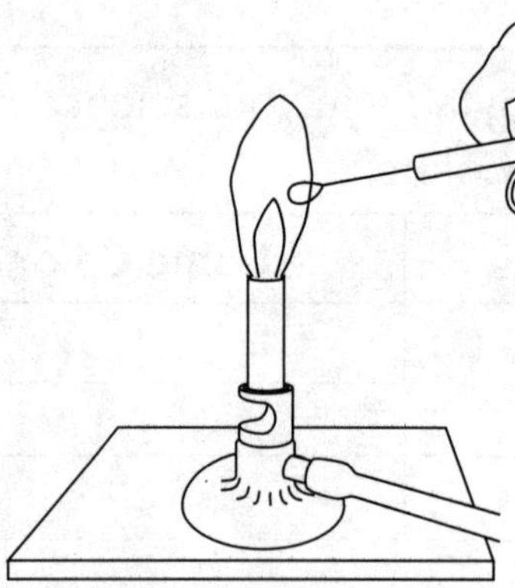

 © Shell Education

Glass

Glass is a material that is made mostly from sand. For practical uses, it is usually clear and transparent. It can be made to be heat-resistant, colored, stronger, more brittle, or more flexible by just changing the amounts of the other chemicals that are added to the silica from the sand. The mixture is heated to a very high temperature so that all the substances melt together. When forensic scientists are asked to compare fragments of glass from a crime scene, there are a number of tests that they may carry out. These include inspection under UV light and a measurement of its density and refractive index.

Some glass samples will fluoresce under UV light, so this test would be carried out first.

Density is a measure of how closely the particles of a material are packed together. If a type of glass contains a lot of lead, then it would tend to be denser than one with very little lead. The density of a sample can be compared by determining in what liquids a sample will float. If the glass is placed in a liquid like water or methylated spirits and it sinks, we know it is denser than these liquids. If it floats on top of a dense liquid like glycerine, then we know it is less dense than glycerine. If the glass neither sinks nor floats in a certain liquid, or mixture of liquids then its density must be exactly the same as the liquid.

If two glass fragments were both suspended in the same liquid, then they would have exactly the same density, and may have come from the same source. Comparison of densities is not used as often in the forensic laboratory today as in previous years, because glass manufactured today is more automated, and density characteristics do not vary as much as they did years ago when each factory had its own "recipe."

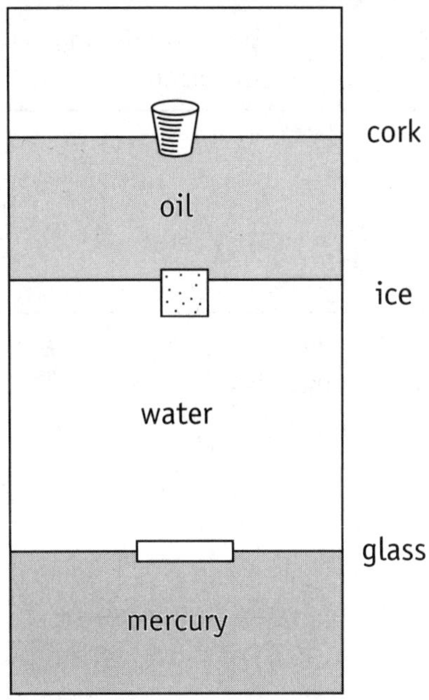

Refractive index is a measure of the amount that light is refracted or bent as it passes out of air and into another transparent substance such as glass or water. This bending of light occurs because its speed is slowed down. The speed of light in air is about 300,000 km per second, while in water it is only about 225,000 km per second. In glass, it is even slower at approximately 200,000 km per second.

Glass (cont.)

The refractive index is actually the ratio of the speed of light through a vacuum to its speed through the material. The refractive index of a vacuum is exactly 1.0, while the refractive index of most glass is approximately 1.5. To determine if two pieces of glass come from the same source, their refractive indices can be compared.

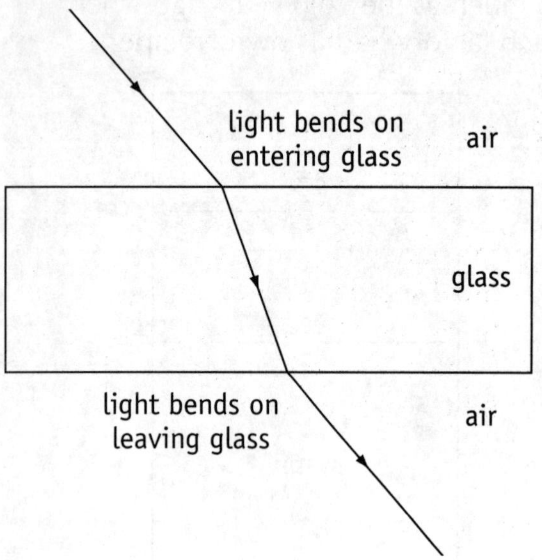

If a piece of glass is put into a dish of water, the outline of the glass can be easily seen because the water and glass have different refractive indices. It is found that some silicone oils have a refractive index slightly higher than that of glass. If the oil is heated, then its refractive index will gradually decrease and become the same as the glass. At that temperature, any glass that is sitting in the liquid will no longer be visible, as the refractive index of the heated oil is the same as that of the glass. If the oil is heated further, then the glass should be visible again as the refractive index of the oil becomes lower than that of the glass.

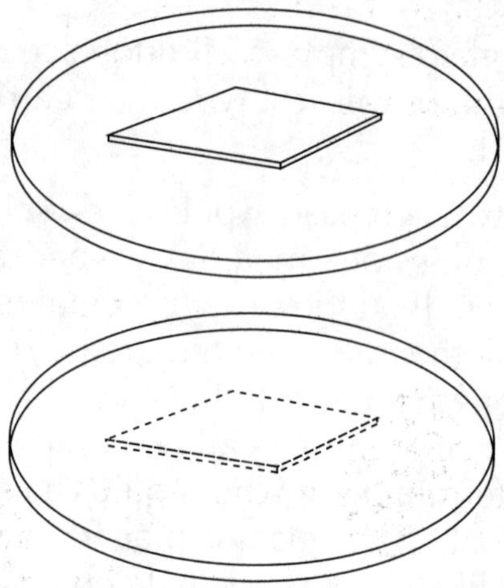

© Shell Education

Glass (cont.)

Comprehension Questions

1. Explain how glass is made. What different properties can it have, and how is this done?
2. Describe three types of tests that are likely to be carried out if you were comparing glass fragments found at a crime scene with others found on a suspect.
3. What is density? What would make some glass samples denser than others?
4. Explain how the density of two fragments of glass can be compared.
5. What is the refractive index of a transparent substance?
6. Describe how the refractive index of two fragments of glass can be compared using a silicone oil whose refractive index is just over 1.5. Explain why this method works.
7. The piece of glass below was found at a crime scene. The three cars A, B, and C were brought in by the police as possibly having been involved in the hit-and-run accident being investigated. From which broken headlight might the piece from the crime scene come?

Missing parts of headlight are shaded.

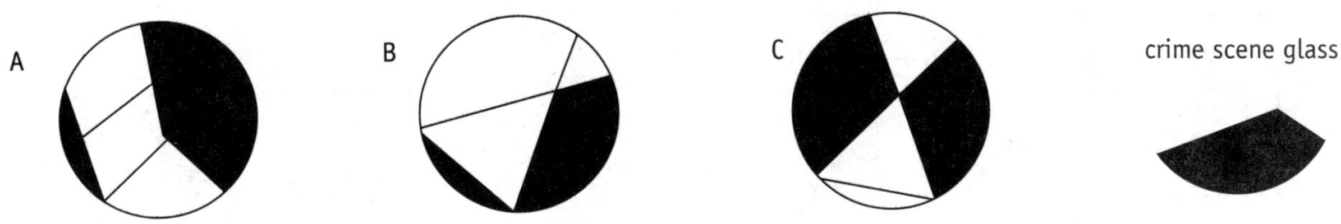

Name ______________________________

Comparing Glass

In this activity you will try to solve a crime that occurred recently when elderly Mr. Ino Scent was attacked and his wallet stolen. In the scuffle, his prescription glasses were broken. A suspect, Miss Vera Lightfingers, was brought in for questioning. Her clothes were searched and a large number of minute glass fragments were found in the seams of her jeans. She explained that these were probably from the glass that she had broken that morning. You have been given the evidence that includes the glass fragments found on Miss Lightfingers's clothes (Exhibit A), glass from Mr. Scent's glasses (Exhibit B), and some glass fragments found in Miss Lightfingers's trash bin (Exhibit C). Your task is to compare the refractive index of the glass samples, and determine if the glass found on the suspect's clothes matches either of the other two samples.

Materials

- petri dish of silicone oil
- tweezers
- three different types of glass samples:
  - (i) glass from suspect's clothes (Exhibit A)
  - (ii) glass from Mr. Scent's glasses (Exhibit B)
  - (iii) glass from Miss Lightfinger's trash bin (Exhibit C)
- hot plate

Procedure

1. Create the following table in your science notebook.

Glass Sample	When Glass Disappeared	When Glass Reappeared

2. Using the tweezers, place the three different glass samples in the oil.

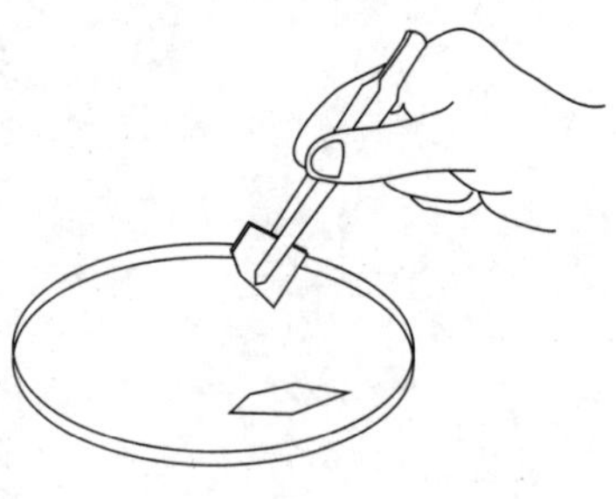

3. Place the petri dish on the hot plate. (Remember which sample is which.)

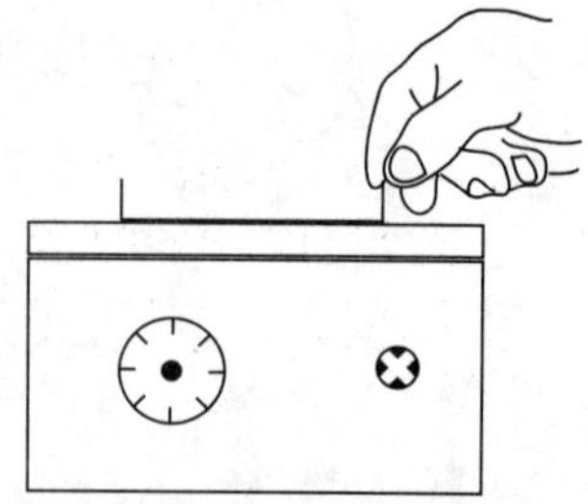

 © Shell Education

Name ____________________

Comparing Glass (cont.)

Procedure (cont.)

4. Gently warm the oil, continuously noting the appearance of the glass fragments.

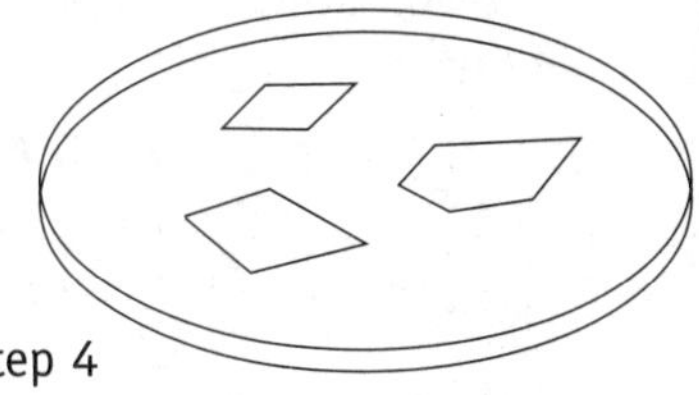

Step 4

5. Record the time at which any of the glass fragments seem to disappear or reappear.

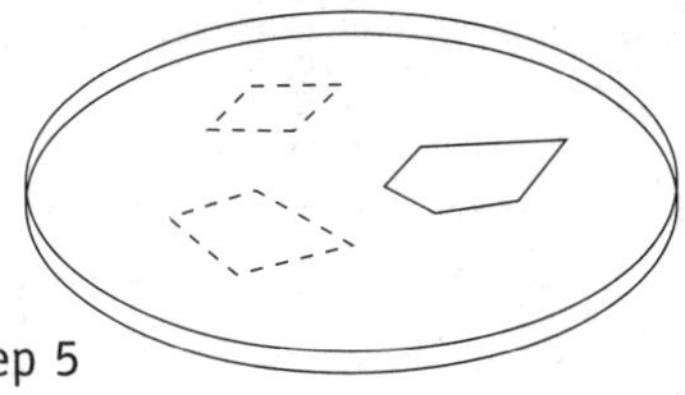

Step 5

Heating glass in silicone oil and recording the temperature at which the glass seems to disappear.

Analysis

1. Did any glass samples disappear and reappear at the same time? If so, which ones?
2. What does this indicate about the glass found on Miss Lightfingers's jeans?
3. As the forensic scientist, what would you report back to the police officers who were investigating this crime? Is the suspect guilty or innocent?
4. Describe any other tests that could be done on the glass to help solve this case.

Soil

Traces of soils are often found at the scene of a crime. Other traces are carried away from the scene on clothing, shoes, and skin; under fingernails; or in the tread of a tire. A small sample of such soil can be analyzed by the forensic scientist to find out where it came from or maybe even what time it was removed or deposited.

Unfortunately, comparing samples of soils may often be inconclusive because there can be differences between soils that are found only a few meters apart. However, soil comparisons can be useful in supporting other evidence, such as footprints and fingerprints.

Soil is made up of small particles of rock mixed with dead and decaying plant and animal remains called *humus*. The rock particles are made of mineral substances that have come from the original rock from which the soil came.

One simple way to identify a soil is to look at its color and compare the sizes of these rock particles. The color of a soil can tell a lot about the minerals in it and is one piece of evidence used by police. It has been estimated that there are nearly 1,100 distinguishable soil colors.

When soil is white or light gray, silica or lime is usually present in its mineral makeup. Black, dark brown, or very dark gray soil is mostly composed of humus. Yellow, brown, and red soils have high concentrations of iron compounds.

Good soils also contain a fair amount of humus. It is the humus in soils that provides nutrients for plants. Humus tends to make soils darker, and it helps soils to remain friable, or crumbly, and moist.

Some common soil types:

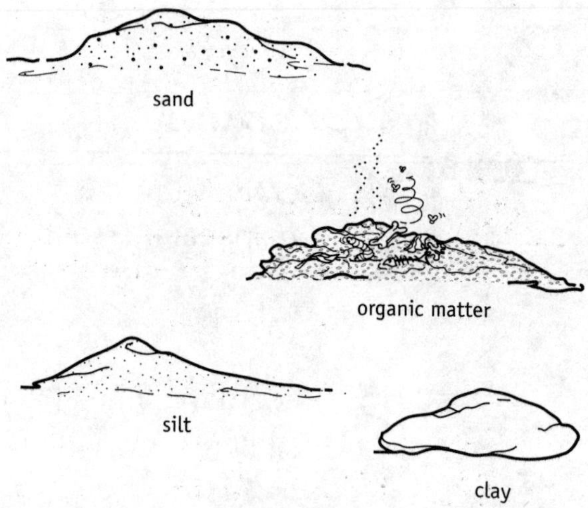

Some organic substances can remain preserved in soil for many years. For example, samples of pollen can remain in good condition for thousands of years. Pollen from plants that have long been extinct has been found preserved in soil.

Comprehension Questions

1. Why is an understanding of soils important to a forensic scientist?
2. What are some of the problems with soil evidence?
3. What are the main ingredients of soil and from where does each come?
4. Name two simple tests that can help distinguish among soils.
5. How does humus help make a good soil?

© Shell Education

Name ______________________

Comparing Soils

In this activity, you will look at a number of different soils and try to determine if any two came from the same place. Be careful: If you are wrong, an innocent person may be incriminated, or your forensic testimony in court may give the real culprit an alibi.

Materials

- samples of soils to be compared
- hand lens
- newspaper

Procedure

1. Copy the following table into your science notebook under the heading "Comparing Soils." Make sure you have enough columns for the number of soil samples you have collected.

Characteristic	A	B	C	D	E
color					
particle size					
organisms					
plants					
dampness					

2. Tip some of sample A onto newspaper.

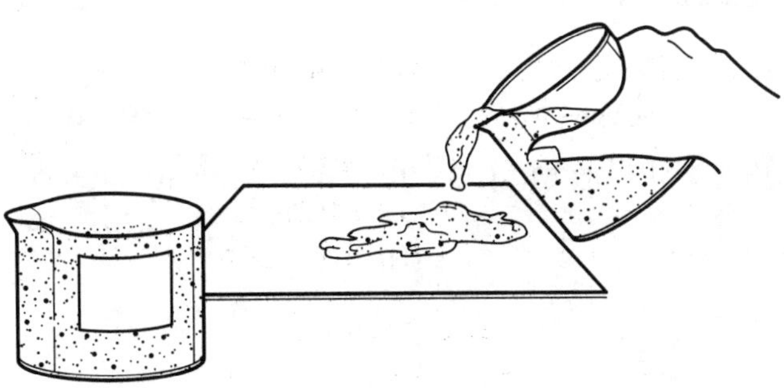

Name ____________________

Comparing Soils (cont.)

Procedure (cont.)

3. Use the hand lens to look for differences in color and particle size in the sample.

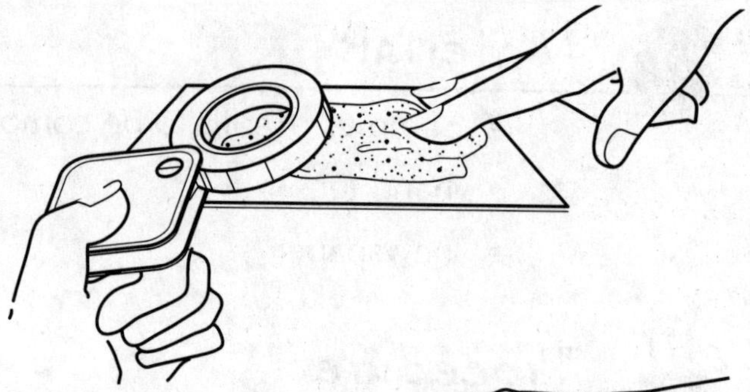

4. Use the hand lens to look for plant and animal matter (twigs, worms, leaves, insects).

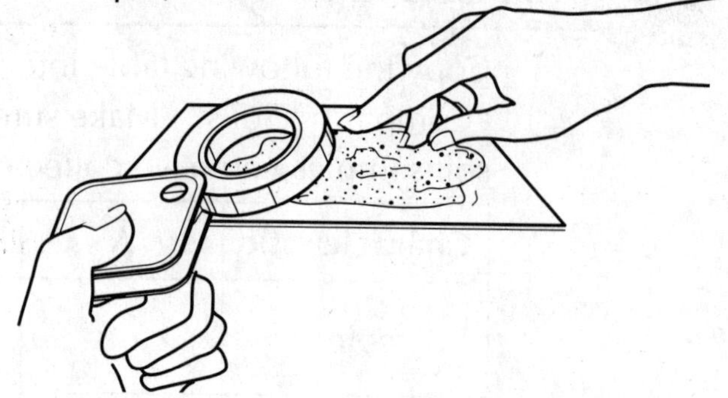

5. Feel the samples to see if they are damp or dry. Record all your findings.

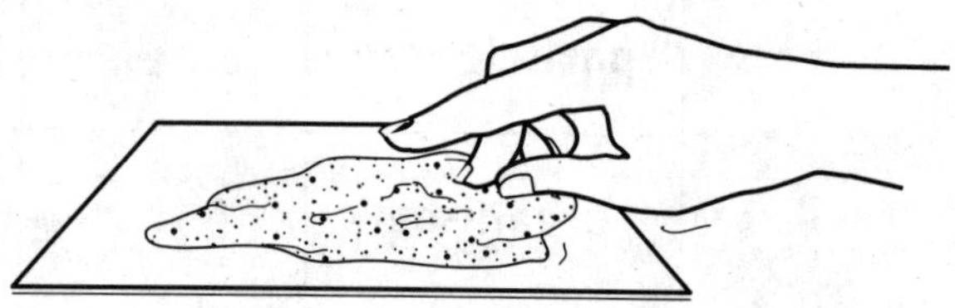

Analysis

1. Describe how each of the soils differed.
2. Do you think any of the samples came from the same place? Give reasons for your answer.
3. Which soil would have been the best for a garden? Explain why you believe this.
4. How could you have improved your observations?
5. What could be the reasons for some samples being damper than others?

© Shell Education

Classifying Soil

Generally, soils can be classified into three main groups depending mainly on the size of the particles.

Sandy Soils

Sandy soils contain a large proportion of sand particles that range from about 0.15 mm to 0.3 mm in diameter. This is large for a soil particle, so it means that the air spaces between the particles are also large. Water drains very quickly through the air spaces in such soils. Unfortunately, this often means that nutrients are also washed away easily.

Sandy soil can be identified by taking a handful of soil and trying to squeeze it together. If the soil crumbles and falls apart, it is considered to be sandy.

particles of sandy soil (diameter 0.2 mm)

particles of clay soil (diameter 0.002 mm)

Clay Soils

Clay soils consist of very small particles, often as small as 0.002 mm in diameter. This means that air gaps are extremely small and water does not drain through very easily. In fact, clay soils are often waterlogged and sticky.

Clay soil can be identified using the same method as for sandy soils. If the handful of soil makes a ball when squeezed together, the soil is considered to be a clay type.

Loam Soils

Loam soils contain many particles that are midway in size between sand and clay. Air gaps are sufficiently small to hold water long enough to allow plant root systems to absorb it, but not so long as to stop the air from getting to the plant roots. Loam soil with plenty of humus is the best type of soil to have in a garden.

Name ____________________

Measuring Soil Particle Size

Materials

- set of sieves
- hand lens
- samples of two different soils

Procedure

1. To accurately measure the proportions of different-size particles in a soil, the soil must be dried and then passed through a set of sieves. First, the soil is shaken through a sieve with large holes so that small particles pass through while large ones are trapped.
2. This procedure is then repeated with smaller and smaller sieve sizes to separate ever-decreasing sizes of particles. The amount of soil trapped in each sieve can be weighed and the proportion of each particle size can be calculated for each soil sample.
3. Copy the table below into your science notebook under the heading "Results." Record your findings.

Sample %	Sample A	Sample B
coarse gravel		
fine gravel		
silt		
clay		
sand		

Analysis

1. Explain how the three soil types differ in particle size and water-holding ability.
2. Describe how you would separate the different-size soil particles to identify the type of soil.
3. Why must the soil be dry in order to measure the size of the particles?
4. Describe how soils A and B differ.
5. Which of the two samples, A or B, would have the best drainage? Why?

 © Shell Education

Name ____________________

Measuring Water in Soil

The differences in water retention of soil can be used to compare samples. In this activity every group of students will dry a soil sample, calculate the amount of moisture in their sample, and compare their results with other groups in the class.

Materials

- soil samples
- evaporating dish
- Bunsen burner
- tripod
- gauze mat
- balance to weigh soil
- metal tongs
- sand bath
- heatproof mat

Procedure

1. Copy the following table into your science notebook under the heading "Measuring Water in Soil."

Soil Characteristic	Before Heating	After Heating
color		
mass		

2. Record the color of your soil, then weigh the empty evaporating dish.

Name ____________________

Measuring Water in Soil (cont.)

Procedure (cont.)

3. Add about 10 grams of soil to the empty evaporating dish and record the mass. Calculate the exact mass of the damp soil.

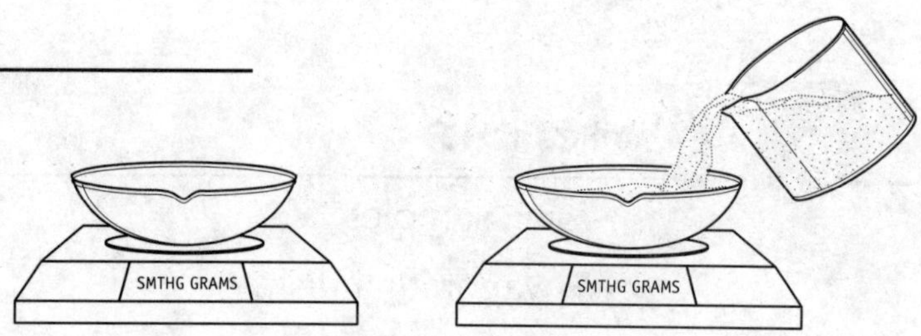

4. Put the dish on the sand bath and heat over a low flame for 20 minutes. Do NOT let the soil burn.

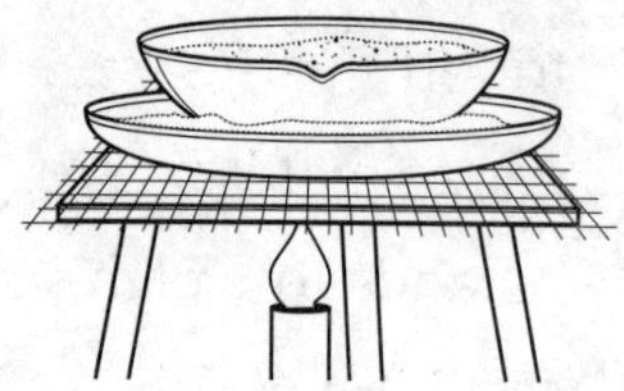

5. Using tongs, remove the dish and place it on a heatproof mat. Leave it to cool, and then record the color of the dried soil.

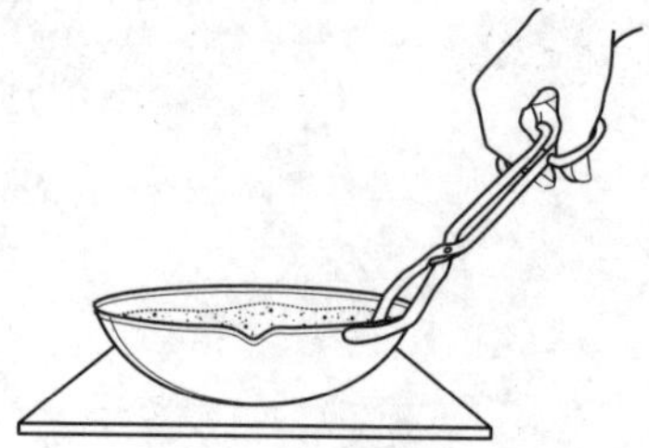

6. Weigh the cooled dish with the dried soil and record this mass in your table.

7. Calculate the amount of water that was lost from the soil and record this to the side of your table.

Analysis

1. Describe what you saw coming from the soil as it was heated.
2. Find the percentage of water in your soil sample by dividing the difference in mass by the initial mass.
3. Draw up a table recording all the class samples, the percentage of water lost from each, and the size of the particles. Which sample lost the most water?
4. Was there any relationship between the size of particles and the percentage of water lost? If so, what did you notice?
5. Compare the appearance of your samples to others in your class. Do you think any of the samples came from the same place as yours?

 © Shell Education

Name ______________________________

Measuring Humus in Soil

If soil is heated enough, not only will the moisture evaporate out, but also all the organic matter, or humus, is burned away. We are left with only the mineral rock particles. We can inspect the colors and proportions of the different rock particles and determine if any may have come from the same place.

Materials

- Bunsen burner
- tripod and gauze mat
- soil sample
- metal tongs
- evaporating dish

Procedure

1. Create a table in your science notebook similar to the table on page 79.

2. Put 5 grams of your soil sample into the evaporating dish. Record its color and mass.

3. Carefully place the dish with the soil sample onto the tripod and gauze mat.

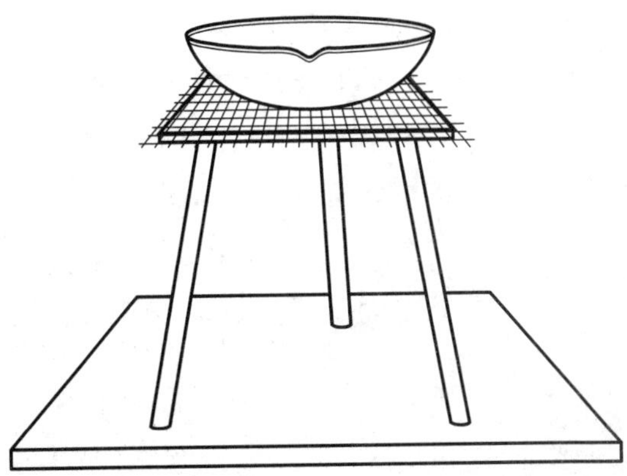

Name ______________________

Measuring Humus in Soil (cont.)

Procedure (cont.)

4. Heat with a high flame for at least 10 minutes. At times, also heat from above.

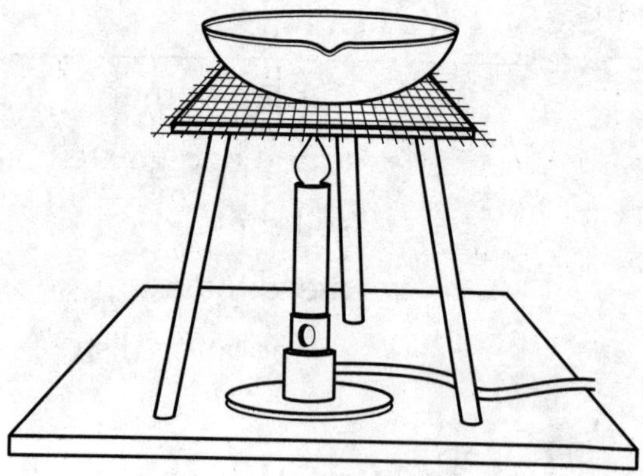

5. Use tongs to remove the dish, and leave to cool. Record the color and mass.

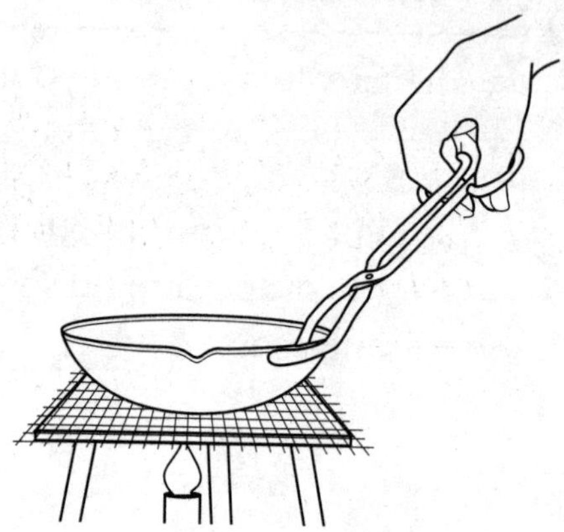

Analysis

1. Describe any observations you made during heating. Use all of your senses.
2. What do you think was burned away?
3. What is the importance of humus to soil?
4. What has been left after the burning?
5. Compare the colors of the other burned soil samples. Do you think any samples probably came from the same place? Explain your answer.

© Shell Education

Soil and Ultraviolet Light

Visible light is only a small part of a large range of radiation waves known as the electromagnetic spectrum. Ultraviolet (UV) light occupies a wavelength band just outside the visible spectrum and cannot be seen by the human eye.

UV light occurs just beyond the visible blue/violet end of the spectrum, which is where the shorter wavelengths, such as X-rays and gamma rays, are found. At the opposite end of the visible spectrum are the red/orange colors, and just beyond human visibility are infrared and microwaves (long waves).

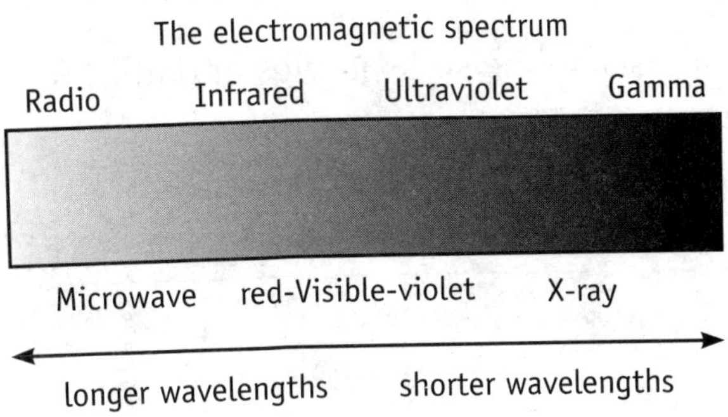

A substance like soil particles absorbs some parts of the visible light spectrum and reflects others. These reflected parts are blended into the color we see. A substance or object also absorbs many of the invisible wavelengths, such as UV. The observation of a substance using a device that can detect ultraviolet light can reveal things not able to be seen with the naked eye.

A trained investigator can use a UV light to find evidence that might otherwise have been missed in natural light. For example, soil particles from different locations that look the same in daylight may appear different when inspected under UV light. A criminal who thinks that they are covering their tracks may not realize the telltale signs that are invisible to their naked eye but can be detected using an ultraviolet detector.

Comprehension Questions

1. How may UV light be useful in solving a crime that involves matching soil samples?
2. Where on the electromagnetic spectrum can UV light be found?
3. Why do we see different substances as different colors?
4. List three other uses for UV light in forensic science, besides comparing soils.

Name ____________________

Comparing Soil under UV Light

In this activity you will view natural and burnt soil samples under a UV light and compare their appearances.

Materials

- ultraviolet lamp
- darkened room or viewing cabinet to exclude as much white light as possible
- soil samples
- burnt soil samples

Procedure

1. Draw a table in your science notebook that lists all the soil samples and allows a space for your observations. Use this as a model.

Soil Samples	Appearance Under UV Light
A burnt A B burnt B C, D, etc.	

2. Examine all the samples under the UV light in the darkened room or cabinet and record your observations.

Analysis

1. Do any soil samples look the same under UV light? What conclusions can you draw from this?
2. Did any samples fluoresce? If so, which ones?
3. Did any of the burnt soil samples differ from their unburnt samples under UV light?
4. Why is UV light a useful forensic tool for examining soil samples?
5. What could have improved your examination of soils under UV light?

 © Shell Education

Acidity Indicators in Soil

Some substances in a soil may dissolve to form an acid or a base. These substances may be a characteristic of that particular soil type, or may be foreign particles in the soil. Garden beds, for example, can have a wide range of topsoils, fertilizers, insecticides, and herbicides added to the local earth. These can spill over, or be carried, into the surrounding soil where their presence may not be expected. Acidity tests can detect differences from the expected norm.

An indicator is a substance that changes color depending on whether it is in an acid, base, or neutral solution. An indicator that is very useful is Universal Indicator, because it can change into a range of colors depending on the strength of the acidity.

This table shows the relationship between pH, color of Universal Indicator, and acidity.

pH	1	2	3	4	5	6	7	8	9	10	11	12	13	14
color			Red	Pink		Orange	Yellow		Green		Blue			Violet
acid/alkaline	←		acid	→			neutral	←			alkaline			→

The pH scale measures from 1–3 (strong acid), 4–6 (weak acid), 7 (neutral), 8–10 (weak base), to 11–14 (strong base). Most soils usually fall into a range of pH 3.5 to 8.5.

The acidity of soil can determine which plants are able to grow in it. Some plants prefer a more acidic soil of pH 3 or 4, while others like the soil to be slightly basic with a pH of about 8. Lime can be added to the soil to raise its pH for basic-loving plants. Fertilizers can be added to soils that are naturally basic, like those formed from limestone, to lower the pH.

Comprehension Questions

1. Copy the pH scale on this page into your science notebook. Using colored pencils, color in the appropriate indicator colors.
2. What sorts of things can alter the acidity of garden soil?
3. What is the range of acidity for most soils?
4. Write a definition for pH that is different from the one given above.
5. Find out which plants like to grow in acid soils and which plants prefer soils that have a high pH.

Soil Case Study

There has been a reported robbery from a house in a residential suburb while the owners, Sam and Ryan Henderson and their only daughter Felicity, age 14, were away on a week's vacation. They left in the second week of February on Sunday morning and returned on the following Saturday afternoon. Some high-end electronics, some expensive jewelry, a camera, and a large sum of cash were missing upon their return. The police discovered that the window to the second bedroom on the first floor had been forced open and the latch broken. The shrubs growing in the garden bed under the window had been partially crushed and there was a trail of small dirt shoe prints on the carpet inside the bedroom.

Sam and Ryan are both avid gardeners with a large developed garden, but they are too busy to spend as much time in it as they would like. They give Shane Masters, a trained horticulturist, a small fee to come over on Thursday, in the second week of every month, to help out. He is a fit young man who enjoys working outdoors even though the job was not very well paid. In this particular week, Shane had fertilized the garden bed, which had changed the soil pH considerably.

While the Hendersons were away, one of their new neighbors, Kathy Simpson, checked the sprinklers on Monday and Wednesday, but reported to police that she had seen nothing unusual. She had also helped out by doing some weeding for them, as she loved gardening herself and admired their garden. She had recently retired, and while she struggled to make ends meet, at least she now had plenty of time to pursue her love of gardening.

You know that the soil from the garden bed under the window was tested and found to be pH neutral on the Thursday before the Hendersons left on vacation. The Crime Scene Investigator (CSI) acted quickly to take soil samples from the footwear of all suspects and from the shoe prints in the house.

Comprehension Questions

1. Soil from Kathy's gardening boots was found to be pH 9. What is the evidence to make her a suspect?
2. Soil from Shane's boots was found to be pH 5. What is the evidence to make him a suspect?
3. Who would be a suspect if the soil samples found in the house tested as highly acidic? Explain your answer.
4. Why did the CSI act quickly to take soil samples?
5. Describe what other information, besides the pH of the soil, would help the CSI to identify the burglar.
6. Visit a garden center and find out what products lower the pH of a soil.

© Shell Education

Name ______________________________

Measuring Soil Acidity

In this activity you will measure the acidity (pH) of a soil sample and compare it to the other samples investigated by the rest of the class.

Materials

- universal indicator
- soil sample
- filter funnel and paper
- retort stand and clamp
- samples of an acid, a base, and water
- 2 test tubes

Procedure

1. Copy this table into your science notebook.

Sample	Indicator Color	pH	Acid, base, or neutral?
soil			
water			
sample acid			
sample base			

2. Put 5 grams of soil into a test tube. Add water to fill the test tube $\frac{3}{4}$ full. Place a thumb on the mouth of the test tube and shake well.
3. Fold a filter paper into quarters. Open it out to form a cone. Set up the filter apparatus as shown.

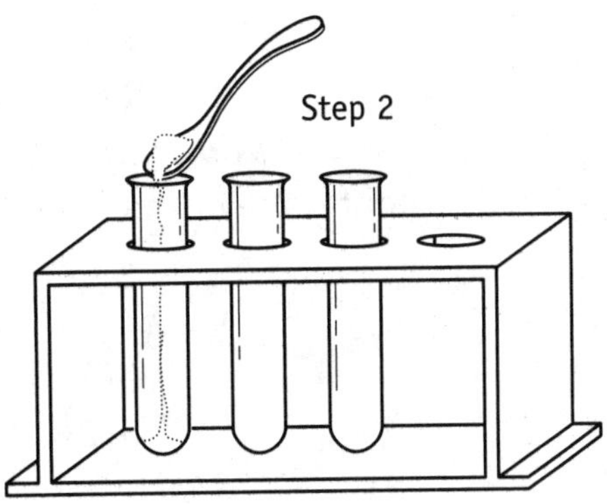

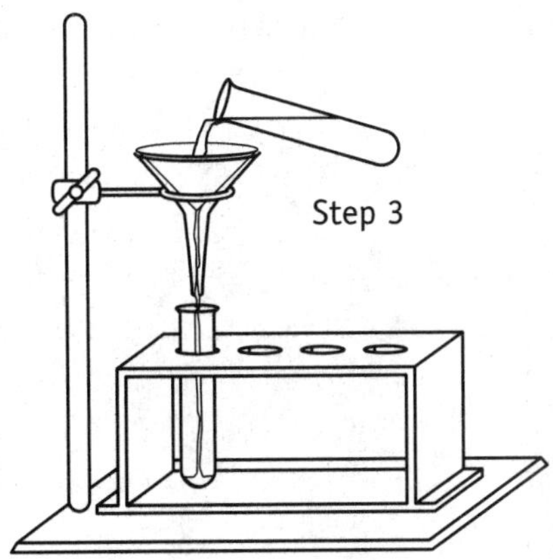

© Shell Education

Name ____________________

Measuring Soil Acidity (cont.)

Procedure (cont.)

4. Pour the contents of the test tube into the filter paper. Watch the clear filtrate slowly drip into the test tube.
5. Place some universal indicator into the filtrate and record color and pH.
6. Test the other three solutions with fresh indicators and also record the colors and pH levels.

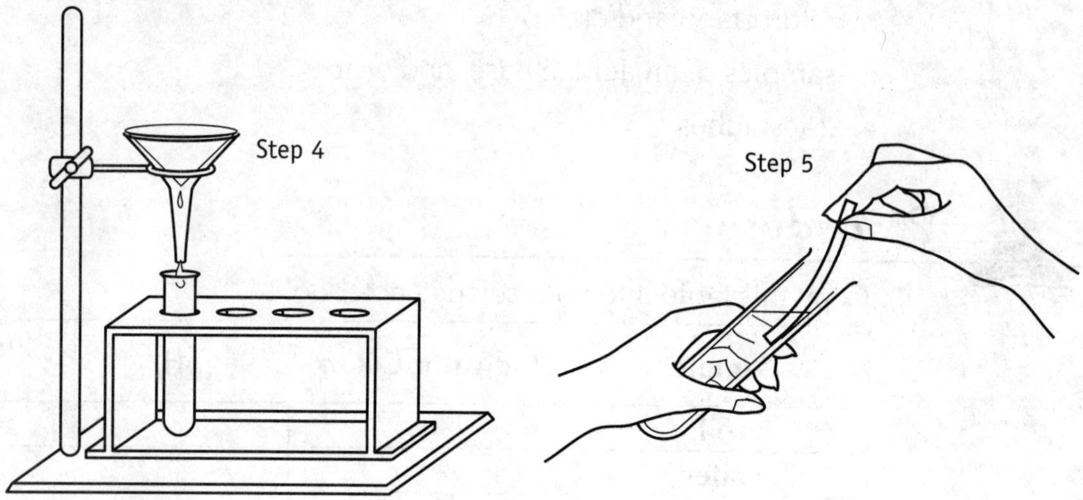

Analysis

1. What color is the universal indicator in an acid?
2. What color is the universal indicator in a base?
3. What is the effect of water on the color of the indicator?
4. Did all the soils tested by the class have the same acidity? If not, what was the range?
5. If tests gave the same result for any two samples, then they may have come from the same place. When all the results were put together, can you determine whether any two soils might have come from the same place? Why do you think this?

 © Shell Education

Fingerprints

Fingerprints are the marks left behind when someone touches an object with their fingers. There are three kinds of fingerprints:

- an impression left in something soft, such as putty, soap, or wet paint
- a print left by a hand covered in dirt, blood, or paint
- an invisible deposit left by the secretions from the skin (small amounts of oil and perspiration are secreted from microscopic pores on the tiny ridges on the fingertips and other parts of the body)

This diagram shows the minute pores in the ridges of the skin through which the sweat droplets emerge.

Sweat glands secrete water, amino acids, salts, and urea through the pores. Oil produced by the sebaceous glands also oozes onto the skin surface. While the water evaporates, the salts, oil, urea, amino acids, and skin debris are left behind in a fingerprint.

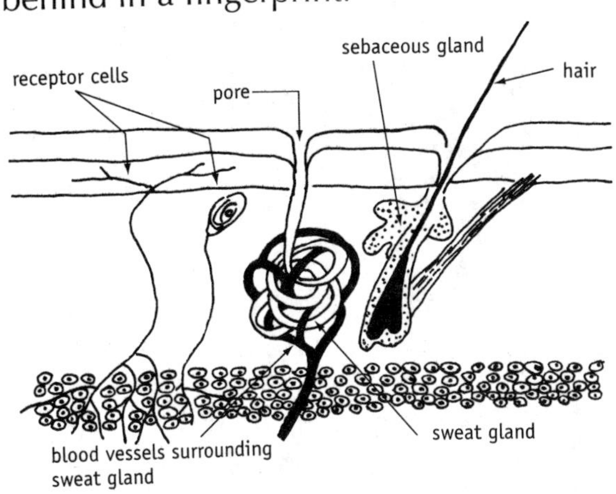

When a soft object is touched, the material it is made of is disturbed and displaced by the person's hand or body. Additionally, whenever anything is touched, a small amount of the body secretions described above is transferred onto that object. The material or secretions are impressed in the same pattern as the ridges on the fingers or palm that made the contact. It is this pattern that makes the distinctive fingerprint pattern.

Every person has his or her own unique pattern of ridges and furrows. They are found on the outer layer of skin of fingers, thumbs, toes, lips, palms, and soles of the feet. There is even a record of a lip print used to identify a car in a hit-and-run accident in the United States.

No two people have the same pattern of ridges, not even identical twins. These patterns are completely formed by the third or fourth month of pregnancy and will never change in shape throughout the person's lifetime. After most injuries and burns, the same patterns will return as the skin heals. Fingerprints are only altered by the most severe of injuries. Then, the injury itself may become as unique and distinctive as the fingerprint it has replaced.

Comprehension Questions

1. Make a list of the three types of fingerprints that may be found at a crime scene and, for each type, write a sentence describing the type of crime and setting where such a fingerprint may be found.
2. Which parts of the body display ridge patterns that allow an impression to be made of them?
3. What are the two glands found in the skin, and what does each one produce?
4. Describe what an invisible fingerprint could be made of, and explain how such a fingerprint is produced on a hard surface.
5. Make a simple copy of the diagram of the skin on page 89, labeling all the main parts.
6. When are a person's fingerprints formed and how may they change or be changed?
7. How many people are likely to have the same fingerprint pattern?

 © Shell Education

Three Patterns of Fingerprints

A person's fingerprints form while still in the womb in the third or fourth month after conception. Before this stage, the fetus has small swellings on the ends of all its fingers and toes. These are called fetal pads. As fetal pads become smaller, the outer layer of skin shrinks and wrinkles slightly to form the papillary ridges and furrows that will become the fingerprint pattern.

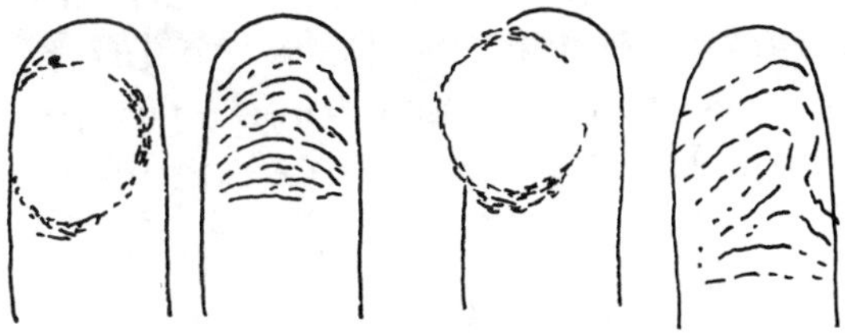

low pad | arch | medium pad | loop

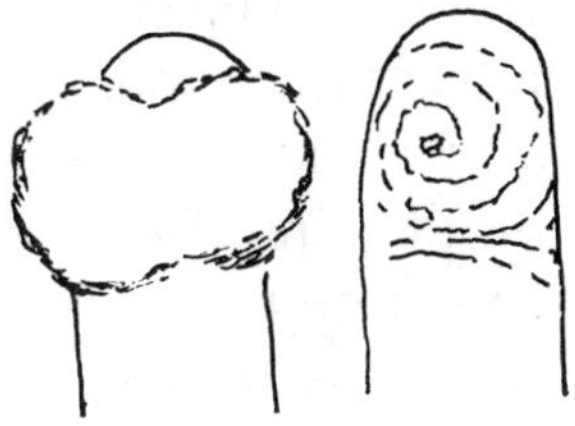

high pad | whorl

Once formed, fingerprints only grow in size as the body grows: the patterns never change, except in the case of severe injury to the lower layers of the skin.

There are three main patterns of fingerprints: arches, loops, and whorls. It has been found that the high swellings in the fetus usually form whorl patterns, the medium swellings form loops, and the low swellings form arches. The height of the swelling also determines the number of ridges as well as the pattern type.

To help identify a fingerprint as one of these three patterns, a triangular shape, formed where two patterns meet, was recognized and called a *delta*. The original three basic patterns were later expanded into the following eight groups using the idea of the delta to help in classification. The core of the fingerprint, found in the center of the pattern, is a second fixed point used to help in classification.

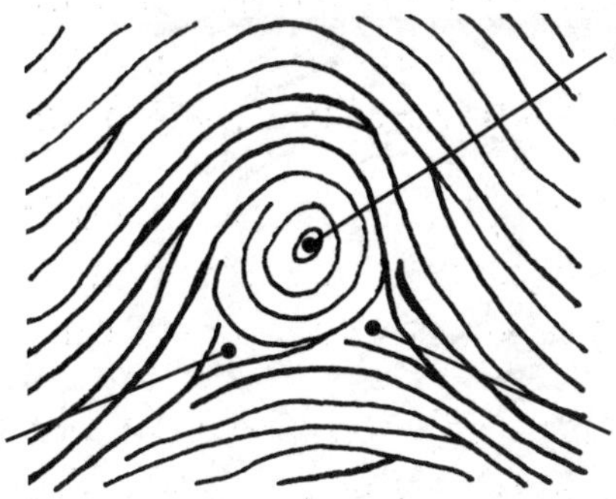

An arch is a pattern that runs from one side of the finger to the other without making a backward turn. Hence, an arch has no delta. A tented arch has an upward ridge that gives the pattern a spine.

arch | tented arch

Three Patterns of Fingerprints (cont.)

When the ridge makes a backwards turn, a loop is formed. A loop has one delta. A loop where the ridges slope downwards toward the thumb is called a *radial loop*, and a loop where the ridges slope toward the little finger of the hand is called an *ulnar loop*.

loop

radial loop on left hand

ulnar loop on left hand

A whorl is a pattern with two deltas where the ridges form a complete turn. A central pocket loop has two deltas. It has a core like a whorl, but the rest of the pattern is like a loop. A double loop has two clear intertwined loops, with two deltas and two cores.

whorl

double loop

central pocket loop

Composite fingerprint patterns are not common. They consist of a mixture of patterns, and may have three or more deltas. These patterns are a complex system of whorls and loops.

Early in the twentieth century, it was found that in Western European populations, the loop was the most common type of fingerprint, accounting for about 60% of all prints. Arches were quite rare, being found in only about 5% of all prints, with whorls and composites making up the last 35% of fingerprints. Loops are also the most common pattern among black Africans and the Ainu people of Japan.

It has been found that among the African Bushmen and Central Europeans, arches are the most common fingerprint, while whorls are more common in the Australian Aboriginal and Mongolian populations. There also appears to be a weak link between a tendency to have high blood pressure and more whorls as well as a link between different blood groups and fingerprint patterns.

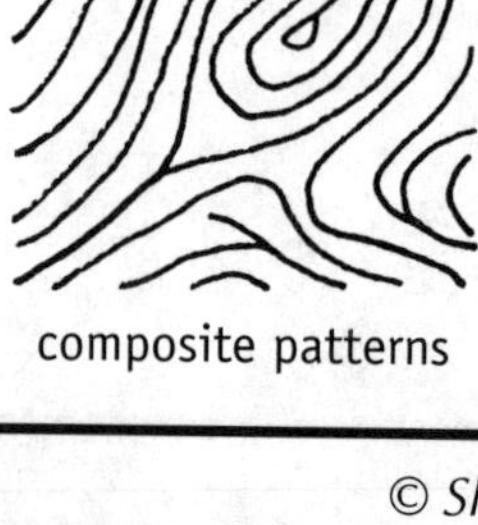

composite patterns

© Shell Education

Three Patterns of Fingerprints (cont.)

Comprehension Questions

1. Make a simple sketch of the eight main fingerprint patterns, naming each type.
2. Explain what the core and delta are, and label them on the diagrams you have drawn.
3. Make a list of the three types of patterns that have one delta.
4. Describe how the patterns of a whorl and a pocket loop are different.
5. Explain how you would decide if a fingerprint is a composite. Sketch an example.
6. In your science notebook, write a paragraph explaining how the papillary ridges form, and how the fetal pads determine the type of pattern that occurs.

Matching Fingerprints

Even considering the eight main fingerprint patterns, it would be impossible to declare two fingerprints to be from the same finger if you were relying purely on matching patterns. So, when matching two fingerprints, it is not the patterns that are important but the characteristics, the little variations that occur in the ridge patterns. For two fingerprints to have been made by the same finger, they must have exactly the same characteristics in exactly the same place.

The table below shows eight examples of such characteristics.

1.	bifurcation or fork	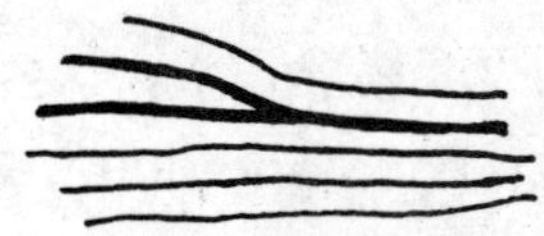
2.	downward ridge ending	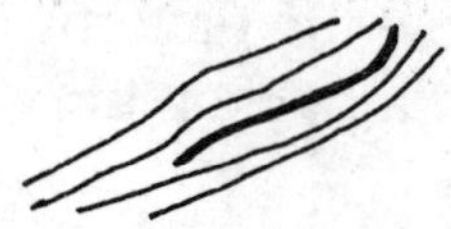
3.	scar	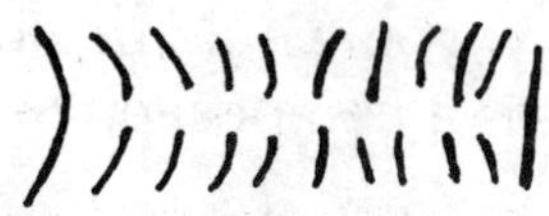
4.	upward ridge ending	
5.	hook	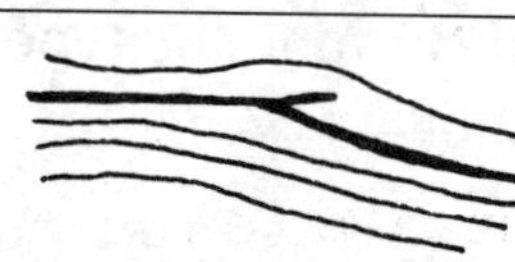
6.	ridge crossing	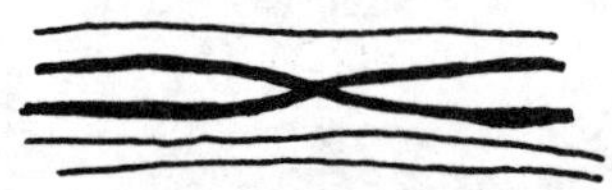
7.	eye or lake	
8.	island	

© Shell Education

Matching Fingerprints (cont.)

In some jurisdictions, there must be a certain number of characteristic points in common if two fingerprints are to be accepted as a match. However, in most jurisdictions there is no minimum number of points of identity required. If a recognized fingerprint specialist declares that, in his or her opinion, two prints are a match, then legally they are accepted as a match. Of course, the greater the number of matching characteristics, the stronger is the print as evidence. Clearly, there needs to be only one single, unexplained difference between two prints for them to be declared not a match.

Comprehension Questions

1. Explain what a characteristic point is, and how a fingerprint expert would use one to try to match a fingerprint found at a crime scene with one on file.
2. To the right are two fingerprints that look the same. Try to find at least 10 possible characteristics in common and label them.
3. Would you say that the two fingerprints are an exact match? If so, explain why you have come to this conclusion.
4. Explain why one fingerprint is a square shape and the other more rounded.

Fingerprinting

Fingerprints are taken using a special inkpad. The fingers are each separately lightly rolled on the ink from one side of the nail to the other, covering the whole of the first joint. They are then carefully rolled on paper on a special form in the place indicated for each finger. This is repeated for all 10 fingers.

All fingers are then printed again together to check the order of the individual prints. Usually whole palm prints are also recorded. Rolled impressions are used because they give maximum detail that may be needed and show the full width of the print.

Whenever a crime has been committed, fingerprints of all people known to have been legitimately at the scene of a crime need to be taken to find which prints may have been left by the criminal. Suspects are also fingerprinted so that they can either be investigated further or be eliminated from further inquiries. These fingerprints are called elimination fingerprints and serve as a "control" against which prints found at the crime scene can be compared.

© Shell Education

Fingerprinting (cont.)

Comprehension Questions

1. Which type of fingerprints do you think would be the clearest: elimination fingerprints, or those found at a crime scene? Explain your answer.

2. Under what circumstances would a person's fingerprints be taken by the police?

3. Why do you think palm prints are also usually recorded?

4. Miss Green had been collecting money for a class party, and had stored it in a cash box left in her desk. The desk was broken into, and the money taken. Some students mentioned that they saw some students from another class acting suspiciously around the classroom at recess, and were able to give the police a good description of those involved. Four suspects were soon found. Their fingerprints and those of Miss Green were taken. The police were also able to get three good thumbprints (A, B, and C) from the cash box. The suspects' thumbprints are shown below.

   a. Which of the thumbprints on the cash box belonged to Miss Green?

   b. Did any of the suspect's thumbprints match thumbprints found on the cash box? Does this mean that this suspect stole the money? Explain your answer.

   c. Explain to whom the third thumbprint on the box may belong.

A B C

thumbprints from cash box

suspect 1 suspect 2 suspect 3 suspect 4 Miss Green

suspect's thumb prints

Name ______________________________

Taking Fingerprints

In this activity you will make a record of your own fingerprints in much the same way the police take those of criminals, suspects, and witnesses. It is a good idea to practice a few times on scrap paper first until you are confident you can get a print that shows the pattern of ridges clearly.

Materials

- newspaper and scrap paper
- inkpad
- soap and towel
- form or paper on which to make the final print
- hand lens

Procedure

1. Place the newspaper on your desk with the inkpad and your record sheet on top of it.

2. Placing your hand near the edge of the desk, roll the end joint of your first finger on the inkpad so that the whole joint is inked. (The illustration shows one finger being rolled.)

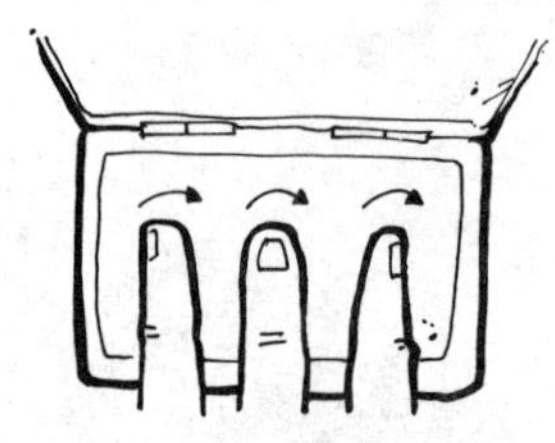

3. Being careful not to use too much ink, which will give a blurred print, roll your finger once only from side to side on your record sheet.

4. Wipe your finger, then repeat with all your fingers and thumb from both hands, making a print of each on your record sheet.

 © Shell Education

Name ______________________

Taking Fingerprints (cont.)

Procedure (cont.)

5. Once you have all your fingerprints recorded, wash your hands well with soap, read the information that follows, and answer the questions.

Race and Fingerprint Patterns

In Western European populations, the loop accounts for about 60% of all prints. Arches are only found in about 5% of all prints, and whorls and composites make up about 35% of fingerprints. Loops are also the most common pattern among black Africans and the Ainu people of Japan. Among the African Bushmen and Central Europeans, arches are the most common fingerprint, while whorls are more common in the Australian Aboriginal and Mongolian populations.

Analysis

1. Copy the following table into your science notebook. Using a hand lens, try to identify the patterns on all 10 fingers. Record the total number of each type of pattern in the table.

Arches	Loops	Whorls	Composite

2. Compare the patterns from your fingers with those of a friend. Are there any similarities?
3. Carry out a class survey and see which patterns are the most common. Add an extra line to the bottom of your table and record the numbers of each pattern in the class.
4. How do these results from your class compare to the figures for the general population? Can you suggest why they may not conform exactly to the national figures?
5. Using your results from the class survey, draw a histogram showing the proportion of each pattern in the class.
6. Using your graph, write a summary of your results, describing how common or rare each pattern is in your class.

Dusting for Latent Fingerprints

Fingerprints made by hands covered in blood, soot, or dirt are clearly visible and can be easily photographed and compared for a match. However, most fingerprints are not obvious. The pattern of salts and oils left behind when the water in the perspiration has evaporated is not easily seen. These are called latent fingerprints, and they have to be developed in some way to make them visible so that they can be photographed. The method used depends on the type of surface on which they are found.

Dusting for Fingerprints

If fingerprints are on a hard or nonporous surface such as glass, glossy paper, or metal, they can be simply dusted with a suitable powder and photographed. The powder sticks to the moist parts of the impression and the loose excess powder is blown or gently brushed away. If the background surface is dark, a white or light powder such as powdered aluminum or talc is used. On white or light surfaces, a dark powder such as carbon is used instead.

After photographing, the dusted print can be lifted with some clear sticky tape. The tape is placed over the print and the powder lifted from the surface. It is then fixed onto paper of a contrasting color. This is just an extra precaution in case the photograph is not clear enough. It can then be kept as a permanent record and compared to other fingerprints already on file.

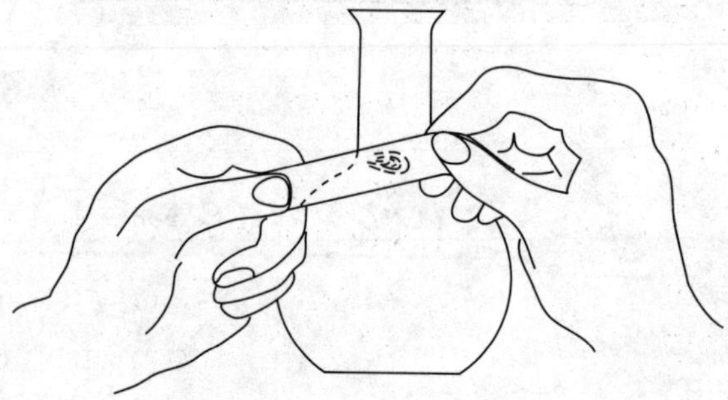

Using Iodine on Absorbent Surfaces

Often a fingerprint leaves oil and perspiration on an absorbent or porous surface, such as cloth or nonglossy paper, that soaks up the fluids, making them unsuitable for dusting. Such latent prints can still be made visible by other means such as iodine vapor.

Today, police often use an aerosol spray of Ninhydrin to develop latent fingerprints on porous surfaces. This chemical reacts with the amino acids left behind in fingerprints. Impressions sprayed with Ninhydrin show up as pink to purple but change to a deep blue when exposed to ammonia.

© Shell Education

Dusting for Latent Fingerprints (cont.)

Teacher Demonstration

This should be done as a demonstration by the teacher, because iodine is corrosive, toxic, and a harmful irritant. The method works because iodine fumes are absorbed by the oil in the impression and leave a brown pattern on the surface.

1. Place a firm fingerprint on a small piece of filter paper.
2. Attach a cotton thread to one end of a paper clip and then attach the paper clip to the filter paper, being careful to not add any further prints to it.
3. Lower the filter paper into a screw-topped jar containing some iodine crystals, as shown in the diagram on the right. Close the lid tightly. If it is a cold day, speed up the sublimation of the iodine crystals into iodine vapor by lowering the jar into warm water. Watch carefully so that you can record your observations.
4. Because iodine sublimes readily in air, the developed fingerprint must be sealed. This can be done by enclosing it completely in sticky tape, or by lowering it into a solution of calcium chloride and potassium bromide for a few minutes.

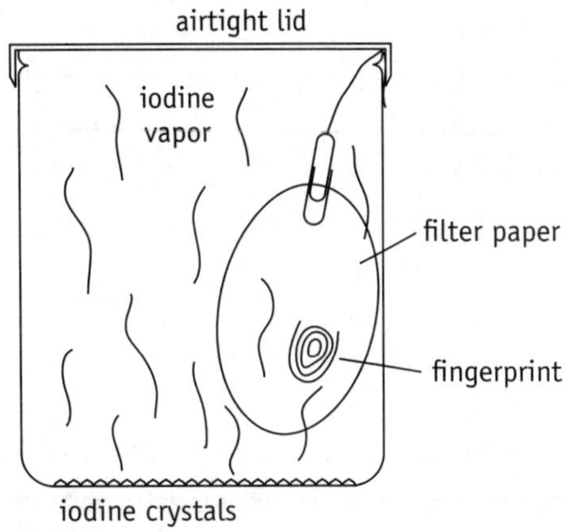

Analysis

Write a short report in your science notebook on what you observed. Record how long it took for the fingerprint to become visible, what it looked like, and what happened to any developed print that was not sealed. Describe how the print was sealed and how successful this was.

Making Fingerprints Visible Using Superglue

Superglue is frequently used at crime scenes to show fresh latent prints on smooth nonporous surfaces. In the presence of water vapor, the superglue leaves a clear white deposit in the pattern of the fingerprint. This activity is best done as a teacher demonstration, as superglue can be quite dangerous if it gets on the skin.

Teacher Demonstration

1. Place a test tube or microscope slide with a fresh fingerprint on it in a plastic lunch box, as shown in the diagram below.

2. In the same box, place a small beaker filled halfway with hot water and a watch glass containing 10 to 15 drops of superglue. Then, seal the lunchbox and place it in a bath of hot water to ensure a humid atmosphere inside the lunch box. You can place weights on top of the lunch box to keep it down in the bath.

3. After about half an hour, open the lid, preferably in a fume cupboard (a ventilated chamber created for this purpose), and you should be able to see a clear white pattern. Fingerprints developed this way cannot be easily lifted but are usually clear enough to be photographed.

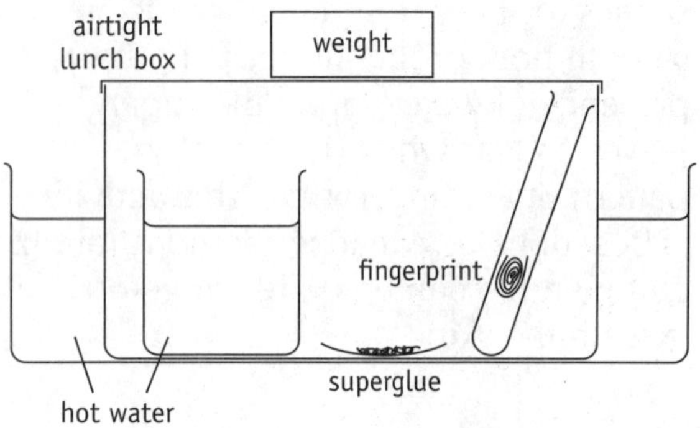

Exercise

Write a report on what you observed and include a scientific drawing of the apparatus used.

Fingerprints on Sticky Surfaces

If fingerprints have been left on a sticky surface such as sticky tape, a bottle, or glass, dusting will not be an appropriate method of revealing such a print, as any dust used would also adhere to the sticky surface. In these cases, another chemical that will remove the sticky surface is used. The chemical is a solution of gentian violet and hydroxybenzene (phenol) crystals in ethanol. This solution is toxic, flammable, and corrosive so care must be taken.

Dusting for Latent Fingerprints (cont.)

Teacher Demonstration

1. Using about eight cm of sticky tape, stick one end around a glass rod and make a fingerprint on the other end.

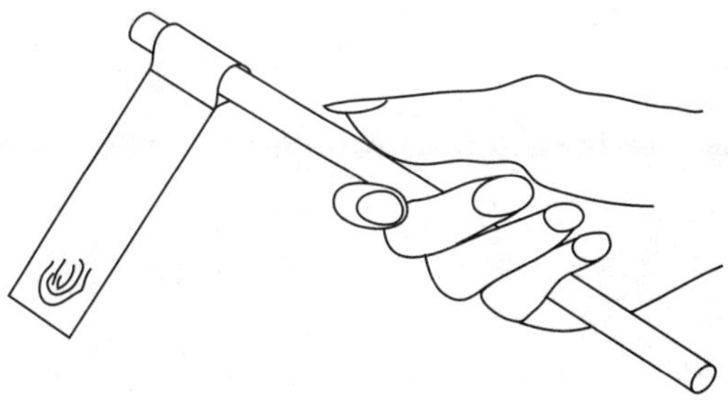

2. Place the entire tape in the gentian violet solution for about 15 minutes. Then, rinse under tap water to remove the sticky surface. Observe the visible fingerprint.

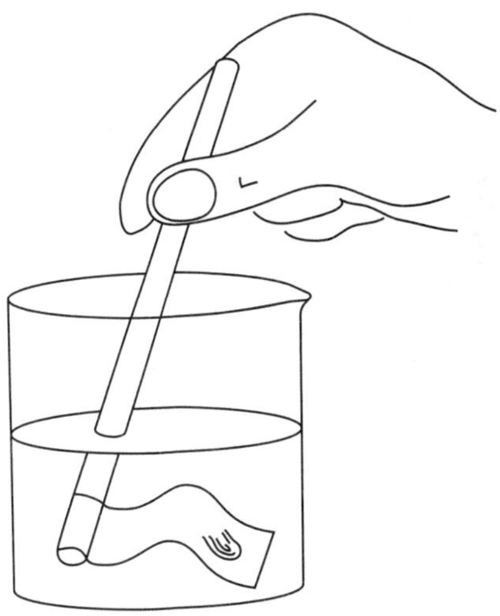

Comprehension Questions

1. What is a latent fingerprint? Explain what has to be done to make them useful in a police investigation.
2. Why are dusted fingerprints lifted if they have already been photographed?
3. With what part of the fingerprint does iodine react?
4. Explain why an iodine print needs to be sealed.
5. Describe the conditions required for superglue to develop a fingerprint.
6. What is the color of the fingerprint left on the tape?
7. What are some sticky objects found at a crime scene that might have fingerprints left on them?
8. Why isn't it appropriate to dust sticky surfaces for prints?
9. Make a list of three places in which fingerprints may be found. Describe the method of developing and recording these prints in each case.
10. Give three examples of some places where fingerprints cannot be easily recorded.

Name ______________________

Taking Latent Fingerprints

In this activity you will make an invisible (latent) fingerprint visible by dusting it with a suitable powder.

Materials

- glossy black paper or plastic
- glossy white surface such as a tile
- talcum powder
- fine carbon powder
- very fine brush such as a makeup brush
- newspaper and tape

Procedure

1. Place some newspaper on the desk to catch any excess powder.

2. Place the glossy black surface on the newspaper and make an impression with a finger or thumb.

© Shell Education

Name ______________________________

Taking Latent Fingerprints (cont.)

Procedure (cont.)

3. Sprinkle some powder of a contrasting color on the area that was fingerprinted.

4. Very gently brush off any excess powder to leave a visible image of your fingerprint. This can be lifted using sticky tape and placed in your science notebook.

5. Repeat steps 2, 3, and 4 with the tile.

Analysis

1. On which surface were the fingerprints most clear?
2. Would this method of dusting prints be suitable for fabric or furry surfaces? Why, or why not?
3. Why would talcum powder be more suitable for dusting than, for example, sugar or salt?
4. What type of powder would you choose to dust fingerprints found on a black ceramic vase? Explain why you have made this choice.

Tool and Tire Impressions

When a burglar breaks into a building or vehicle, marks are usually left behind on any window or door that may have been broken or forced open using a tool. When driving over soft ground, the tires of a vehicle leave impressions in the ground. Moving on foot may leave footprints, or more correctly, shoe prints. A great deal of information can be gained from the marks a burglar leaves behind.

Tools such as screwdrivers, chisels, saws, or knives may look the same as any other, but each gets knocked and scratched in different ways in its lifetime. The marks on its blade may be almost as good as a fingerprint for identifying it later.

Like tools, tires acquire unique marks. Cuts, embedded stones, or uneven wear each give the tire its own characteristics. By examining the impressions left by a tire, a forensic scientist can tell in which direction the vehicle was traveling and whether it kept moving or stopped in one place for a while, and even an estimate of its speed may be revealed.

Marks on a screwdriver tip

Tire prints in soft soil

Comprehension Questions

1. Name a utensil found in the kitchen that could leave scrape marks.
2. List three tools around the house that could be identified by their unique blade marks.
3. List three distinguishing marks on the tire in the photo above.
4. Identify three implements in the science lab that could be traced by their scrape marks.
5. What type of scrape marks might a burglar leave at a house robbery?

© Shell Education

Preserving Impressions

When an object is pressed into soft ground, it will leave behind a negative mold of itself, including any marks or imperfections it might have. Signs of wear and damage or the maker's brand name may be visible. However, prints found in soft ground are easily destroyed by other feet, cars, or weather. Hence, they must be permanently preserved for future reference. The main aim in collecting any impression evidence at a crime scene is to preserve it for later examination in the forensic laboratory. At a later date, it may make a possible appearance as evidence in court.

A photograph is the first step in preserving an impression. In addition to a shot from overhead, photographs are taken from as many angles as possible so as to retain the maximum information.

A clearly marked ruler should always be laid beside the print as a guide to the scale, in case the photographs are ever enlarged or reduced. The ruler should be placed so that it clearly does not block any part of the impression.

In addition to photos using natural lighting or automatic flash, several shots should be taken with an angled light source. If the light comes from one side, the peaks and troughs cast shadows, which will show the pattern more clearly.

Photos of the same impression using a variety of angles and lighting directions

Preserving Impressions (cont.)

Comprehension Questions

1. Describe the information that a crime scene investigator could get from the impression of a shoe print at a crime scene.
2. Explain how a vehicle tire print would be useful to the forensic investigator.
3. Why must impressions be preserved?
4. What is the first step in preserving an impression?
5. List any features that could distinguish the front tires from the rear tires on your family car.

© Shell Education

Making a Cast

Making a cast is another way a permanent record may be made of an impression. This is important in the case of a trial to help the jury to understand exactly what was found at the scene of the crime. A physical three-dimensional cast may be a lot easier for untrained jurors to analyze than flat photographs or a mere verbal description. A photograph may also be unclear in lighting or depth perspective.

The choice of materials used for making the cast will depend on a number of things, including where the impression is, under what conditions the material will set, and how much detail is required. All materials used for making casts have their own properties that make them more or less suitable in each case that a cast is needed.

Casts of fairly large impressions on horizontal surfaces can be made using plaster of Paris (or one of the modern quick-setting materials now available). The accurate copy of the surface and size of the original object that is made can then be sent to the laboratory and compared with any suspect object.

In many cases, plaster of paris is used because it is cheap, safe to handle, and easy to prepare. However, it is not always the most suitable material. Plaster of Paris is calcium sulfate monohydrate. When it is mixed with water, it expands slightly and gets warm as it sets. It is also used in a thick, runny consistency and takes around 48 hours to set. This means that it does not work well for prints in snow or ice, or on nonhorizontal surfaces. However, it is most suitable for footprints found in a flowerbed, under a window where a criminal has broken in, or for tire impressions. Providing that the plaster mix has no lumps or bubbles and is runny without being too thin, it will flow into all parts of the impression to give a suitable cast of sufficient detail.

In the case of a much smaller and detailed tool mark, which may be at any angle on an object such as a door lock, window, or safe, a pad of quick-setting plastic is more appropriate. The plastic is pushed firmly into the indent; then, when the plastic sets, it can be peeled away. An impression of the mark is cast into the plastic. Modeling clay will give similar detail, but is more easily destroyed. Tools found by the police can be compared to the impression. If done correctly, the tool used to make the mark should match the plastic cast exactly.

Comprehension Questions

1. What makes a cast an important piece of evidence in court?
2. Where is quick-setting plastic more appropriate than plaster of Paris for making a cast?
3. How would you decide which casting material to use?
4. Why is plaster of Paris not suitable for use in snow?

Casting Material Characteristics

Ideally, a casting material should be:

- cheap
- easy to prepare and use under poor weather conditions and in remote places
- able to set quickly
- able to make a clear, detailed, and accurate cast

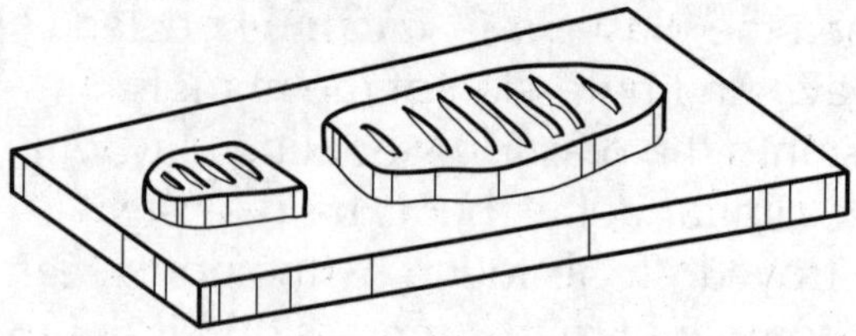

example of a good cast

The casting material should NOT:

- shrink or expand during or after setting
- stick to the impression
- damage the impression when removed
- be hazardous to use

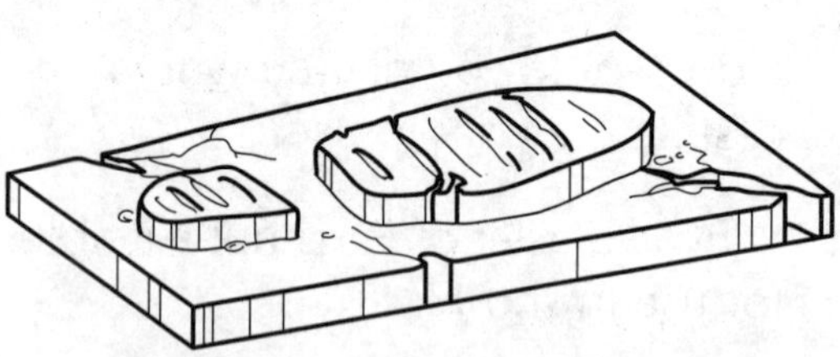

example of a poorly prepared cast

The choice of casting material depends on the following:

- the size of the impression and number of impressions required (i.e. needs to be inexpensive if large quantities are needed)
- the material that the impression is in (e.g. soil, snow, sand, metal, glass, stone, or wood)
- whether the print is made on a horizontal, vertical, or sloping surface
- whether the impression can be kept undisturbed for any length of time after the cast has been pored (i.e. security from damage)
- whether it matters if the original impression is destroyed during casting
- the local environment that the impression is in (i.e. extremes of temperature or exposure to the weather)

There are several materials for making casts and impressions that are in common use in forensic labs around the world. However, new materials and techniques are continually being discovered and tested. Many have properties that make them excellent for a specific task or a particular location.

© Shell Education

Casting Material Characteristics (cont.)

Examples of Casting Materials

The three products described below are commonly used by crime scene investigators and are widely used internationally.

Plaster of Paris or Dental Stone

This is cheap and suitable for larger impressions such as footwear marks and tire prints. It is not suitable to use if the impression is not on a horizontal surface, as the mixture would run out before it is able to set. It is also not suitable if the impressions are only small scratches and great detail is needed. The powdered plaster is mixed with water into a thick creamy paste. As it sets, the plaster gets warm and expands very slightly. This is why plaster of Paris does not work well in snow or ice, as the heat would melt the mold before the cast set. Dental stone is very similar to plaster of Paris and is used by many crime scene investigators because it sets very quickly.

Silicone Rubber or Plastic

These are relatively new materials that are now used routinely when more detail is required than can be obtained with plaster of Paris or dental stone. They are more expensive than other casting materials but set very quickly, and so are often chosen in difficult situations such as sites exposed to bad weather. They are used almost exclusively on tool marks where very fine detail is needed.

Graphite and Sulfur

This is a mixture that was often used for casting scratches in metals or when a casting was required on wet ground or in snow. The mixture melts easily on heating and solidifies very quickly. It is able to give great detail on things like scratches on metal and even the fingerprints in modeling clay, if modeling clay is used to make a mold to contain the liquid mixture. Care must be taken to heat the mixture gently, preferably in a sand bath, to ensure that the sulfur does not produce a vapor that can catch fire and produce poisonous sulfur dioxide fumes. It is not recommended this be done anywhere but in a fume cupboard. Today synthetic silicon-based casting materials have almost completely replaced this mixture.

Comprehension Questions

1. Why should a casting material be easy to prepare?
2. How is shrinking, during or after setting, a problem for a cast?
3. Name one large and one small impression that may be found at a crime scene.
4. What are the conditions in which plaster of Paris would not be a suitable casting material?
5. When would you use silicone rubber instead of plaster of Paris?

Name ______________________

Making a Cast

In this activity you will make a cast of either a car or bicycle tire print, shoe print, or handprint using plaster of Paris. The class should make at least three shoe casts, which can then be used again in other activiies.

Materials

- box of damp sand
- plastic ice cream container or something similar in which to mix the plaster
- old spoon and paper clip
- plaster of Paris
- newspapers and a strip of cardboard to make a mold

Procedure

1. Lay some newspapers on the floor and place a tray of damp sand on them.

2. Make a shoe or tire print in the sand.

© Shell Education

Name ______________________________

Making a Cast (cont.)

Procedure (cont.)

3. Place about 70 mL of water in a plastic beaker or container.

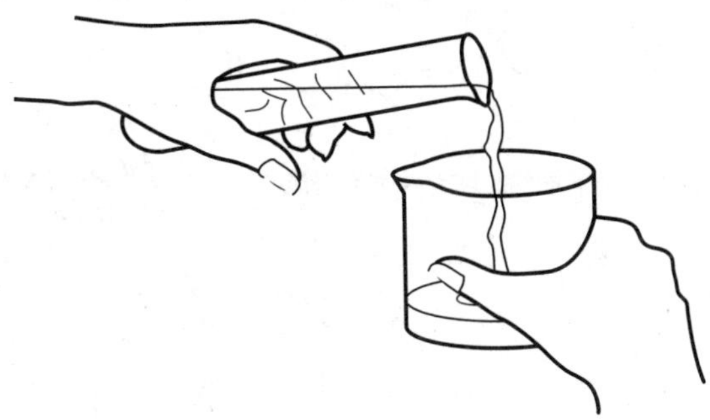

4. Fill a dry 1 L beaker with plaster of Paris (30 mL of salt optional).

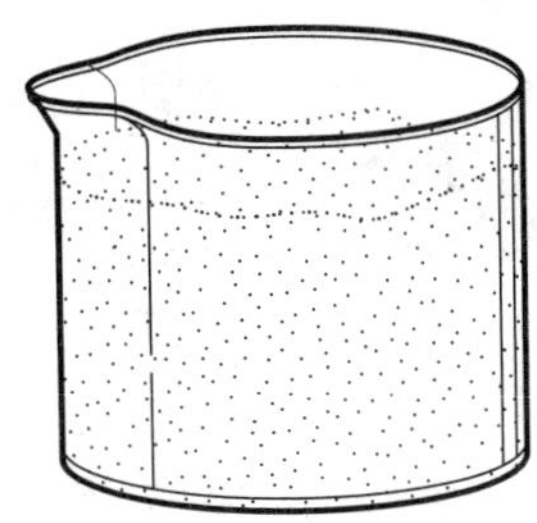

5. Make a mold around part of the shoe print with a strip of cardboard. Hold the mold together with a paper clip.

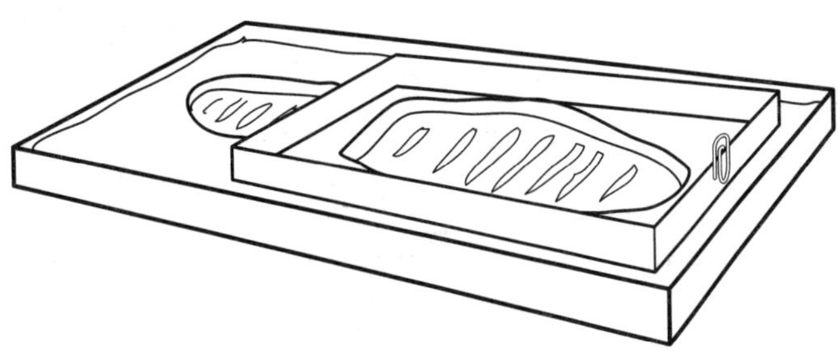

Name ______________________

Making a Cast (cont.)

Procedure (cont.)

6. Pour the plaster and salt into the water and mix until you have a thick, creamy mixture.

7. Pour the mixture into the mold. Let the plaster set overnight or longer, then lift the plaster out carefully.

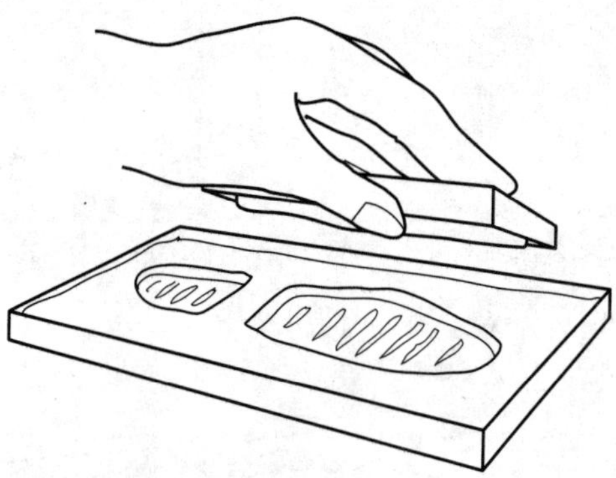

8. Rinse your cast clean under the tap or brush.

 © Shell Education

Name ______________________________

Making a Cast (cont.)

Analysis

1. Make a sketch of the pattern of your cast in your science notebook. Do you think that the cast is an accurate copy of the mold? Explain your answer.
2. Explain in one paragraph how plaster of Paris is prepared for making into a suitable casting material.
3. Why is it important to brush and wash the plaster cast clean of sand before examining it?
4. Why should you avoid having air bubbles in the plaster mixture?
5. Which of the following impressions would give a good plaster cast? Give a reason for your answer in each case.

   a. bicycle tire print

   b. scratches on a stone floor

   c. shoe print in soft soil

   d. marks on a desktop

   e. shoe print in snow

   f. tractor tire print

   g. scratches on a bullet

   h. fabric impression on some putty

Footprints

Critical information can be gained from footwear marks (footprints) left at a crime scene. All people walk differently. Their individual walking styles wear out the soles and heels of their shoes differently.

A burglar carrying stolen goods will leave deeper footprint impressions because of the extra weight of the stolen goods. There will be a difference in the prints if the stolen goods are carried by the arms in front of the body or, for example, in a backpack.

The prints will also change if a culprit is chased or is disturbed and changes from walking to running. When jogging, the prints will be slightly farther apart than at walking pace, but the weight will still be on the heels. A person sprinting will change his or her weight to the balls of the feet and so the front of the impression will be deeper. When sprinting, the heel impression will be reduced or will disappear altogether. The distance between prints will also be further apart than at jogging speed.

If injured and limping, a person's shoe prints will be uneven, with one foot leaving a clearer and deeper impression than the injured foot, which may leave only a partial or very light impression. An injured person will try to put as little weight as possible on the injured foot.

Comprehension Questions

1. Which footwear mark below would most likely belong to a criminal carrying heavy stolen goods away from a crime scene? Explain why.

© Shell Education

Footprints (cont.)

Comprehension Questions (cont.)

2. Which footwear mark below would most likely indicate a person running away? Explain why.

3. In the photos from the previous two questions, which person is walking? How can you tell?

4. Sketch an outline of your shoe. Draw in the patterns on the sole, and the wear marks that are unique to your shoe.

5. Compare your drawing for question four to that of your neighbors. List all the differences.

Name ____________________

Comparing Footprints

For this exercise you are required to compare and match the footwear marks found at three crime scenes with the shoes collected from the addresses of five different suspects. You will have three test impressions (plaster casts) of shoe prints found at various burglary scenes and five photographs of the seized shoes.

Materials

- three test impressions of shoe prints
- five photographs of "seized shoes"
- hand lens
- ruler

Procedure

1. Using a ruler and hand lens, inspect the prints for individual characteristics and determine which suspect's shoes made the marks at each crime scene. Copy and complete the table below.

Crime Scene Shoe Print	**Suspect Shoe 1, 2, 3, 4, or 5**
A	
B	
C	

Analysis

Explain how you reached the conclusion that enabled you to fill in the table.

 © Shell Education

Name ______________________

Evidence in Shoe Prints

Footwear marks can tell a crime scene investigator a lot about how the person was moving and whether anything was being carried.

In this activity you will investigate how shoe prints vary under five different circumstances. If a burglar breaks in through a window, shoe prints may be left in the soft soil of a garden bed.

Materials

- sandpit and rake
- a measuring tape or meter ruler
- heavy school bag
- volunteer to walk and run across the sandpit

Procedure

1. Draw the following table in your science notebook as shown below.

How Shoe Prints Were Made	Distance Between Prints	Depth of Toe	Depth of Heel
walking			
running			
limping			
carrying bag in front			
carrying bag on back			

2. Rake the sandpit smooth, watering it if it is very dry.

Name ____________________

Evidence in Shoe Prints (cont.)

Procedure (cont.)

3. Have the volunteer walk slowly and naturally across the sand.

4. Inspect the resultant shoe prints and calculate the average distance between the prints.

5. Inspect and record the depth of both toe and heel imprints.

 © Shell Education

Name ______________________

Evidence in Shoe Prints (cont.)

Procedure (cont.)

6. Rake the sandpit again and complete the table with the volunteer running, limping, and carrying a heavy bag both in front and on the back.

Analysis

1. Under what circumstances was the distance between shoe prints greatest?
2. When were the heel prints deepest?
3. When were the deepest toe prints obtained?
4. What was the effect on the prints if a heavy load was carried?
5. What difference did it make if the load was carried on the front?

Name ______________________________

Determining Events from Snow Tracks

Materials

- copies of the picture below, one per student

Procedure

1. Distribute copies of the picture.
2. Explain to the students that the tracks in the snow tell a whole story. This is Prince Road, half an hour after the accident that later made headline news in the local newspaper.
3. Have the students study the picture carefully and then answer the questions.

Analysis

1. Can you work out what happened? Write out in list form the chain of events in this scenario.
2. How many people were involved?
3. What animals were involved?
4. How many vehicles were there?
5. Could this accident have been prevented? How?

 © Shell Education

The Characteristics of Tools

Tool marks can include impressions from a screwdriver, chisel, or crowbar, cut marks made by wire cutters or a saw, or scratch marks that could be made by a knife or other sharp instrument scraping over a surface.

These marks can provide important information to an experienced investigator, and can possibly lead to the identification of the implement that made them. The item might then link a possible suspect to the crime scene.

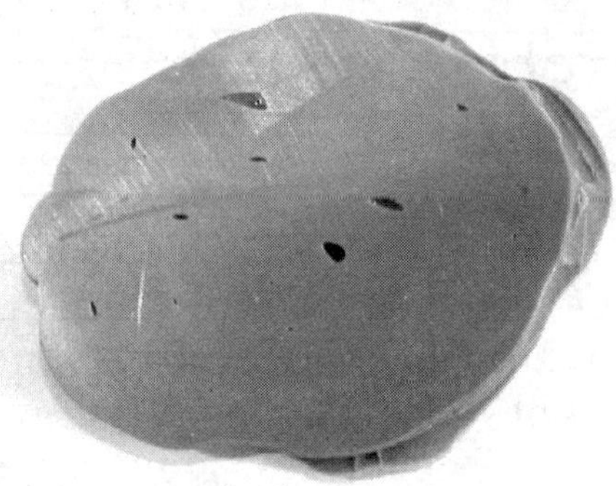

Cast made of a tool mark left by a chisel

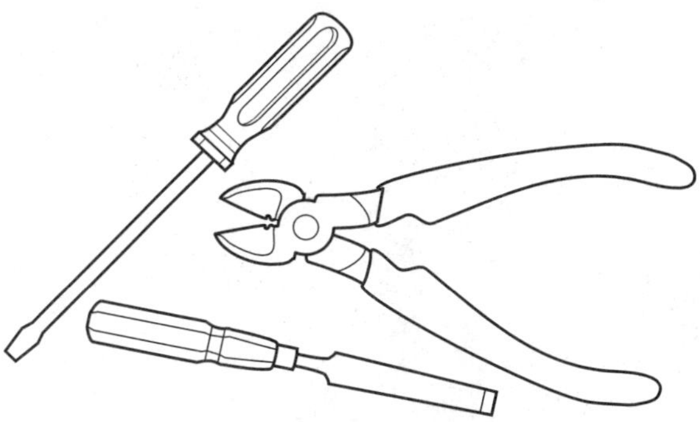

One tool mark that is commonly found at forced entries is caused by a crowbar, chisel, screwdriver, or other easily accessible tool getting wedged between a wooden doorjamb and a door or between a window and its frame. The much harder metal compresses the wood, leaving an impression of its shape behind.

Notice in the picture to the right how the small nicks and breaks on the end of the screwdriver match the impression. This individualizes the tool to that particular mark.

Matching a tool mark to a tool

Other screwdrivers of the same type would not be expected to have exactly the same little nicks in exactly the same places and be of exactly the same shape. Most metal tools acquire their own unique individual marks through general wear and tear. It is these marks that can link one particular tool with a crime scene or to an owner. If matching marks cannot be found on a suspect's own tools, then it may actually help in proving innocence.

The Characteristics of Tools (cont.)

Matching a Mark to a Tool

If the edge of a tool is scraped against a softer surface, it may cut a series of striated lines that reflect the pattern of the tool's edge. In the laboratory, markings left in this way are compared with test tool marks made with the suspect tool using a comparison microscope. When sufficient striations match between the marks found at the crime scene and the test markings, it is declared a positive comparison.

The photograph below shows some striations found at a crime scene being compared with some test markings done with a suspect tool under the comparison microscope. This example shows a positive comparison between tool and marks on either side of the broken line.

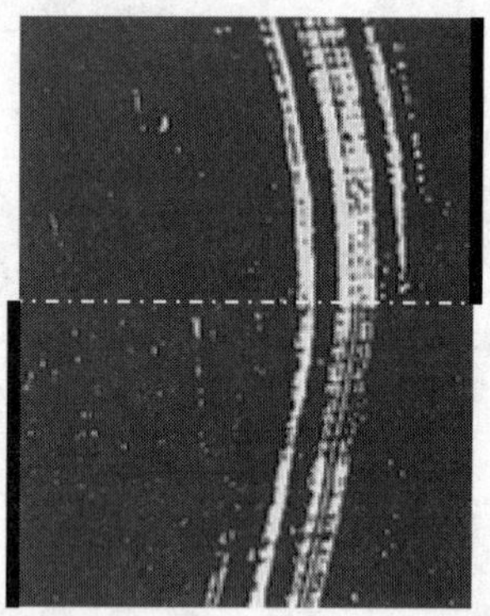

Matching tool marks under a comparison microscope

The Characteristics of Tools (cont.)

Comprehension Questions

1. Under what circumstances might tool marks be left at a crime scene?
2. Explain in what way tool marks might be useful in a forensic investigation.
3. What can give tools their own unique marks?
4. What limitations are there in the use of tool impressions?
5. What casting material would be most suitable for making a cast of a tool impression? Why?
6. A tool mark found at a crime scene where a window had been forced open was thought to have been made by a screwdriver. The crime scene investigator (CSI) made a cast of the mark shown to the right. The other four marks were made by the CSI who was testing some tools found near the crime scene, which may have been used by the burglar. Which tool mark to the right most closely matches the marks left at the crime scene?

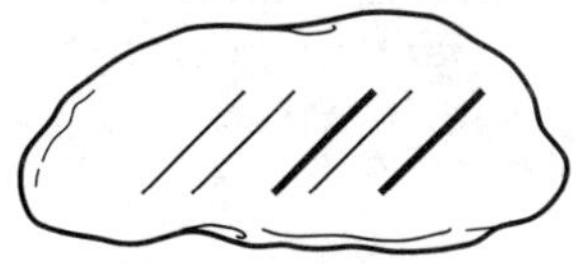

crime scene

a 

b 

c 

d 

Name ______________________

Comparing Tire Marks

In addition to being able to identify a suspect by matching shoes or car tires to impressions left at a crime scene, these marks can also provide a wealth of other information about the person or vehicle.

If a vehicle has left good clear tire marks, they can show both the direction of travel and maybe even the vehicle's approximate speed. Tire prints can reveal the specific tire brand and model by each manufacturer's unique tread pattern. Other obvious features include width and depth of tread. Wear to particular areas of the tire can indicate hard driving, incorrect inflation pressure or incorrect wheel alignment or balance.

Materials

- bicycle and volunteer rider
- some muddy ground
- hand lens

Procedure

1. The volunteer should ride the bicycle across the muddy patch of ground slowly in one direction, then return making a second set of tracks in the opposite direction.
2. Using the hand lens, inspect the prints, taking careful note of the appearance of the impressions.
3. Repeat the same procedure as above but with the bicycle being ridden at a much faster speed. Again inspect the tops of the impressions with a hand lens.
4. Repeat with the rider going as slowly as possible, and note the tops of the impressions and the line of the two wheels.

Analysis

1. In which direction are the tops of the impressions pulled?
2. Describe the effect of speed on the appearance of the tops of the impressions.
3. When the bicycle was going slower, describe how the patterns made by the two tires differed from when they were moving faster.
4. Draw line diagrams of your findings and label each of the three different speed impressions.
5. Are there any other differences to the three impressions besides the tops?

© Shell Education

Difficult Casting Situations

Sometimes, a tool mark may be in a door or window frame that is not horizontal. A liquid casting material cannot be used in this case, as it would just run out before it can set.

Plaster running out of impression in doorjamb

Something like modeling clay, which can be pushed into the indentation, is required. Unfortunately, modeling clay always remains soft, and it is usually bent out of shape when being removed from the mold.

Modeling clay distorts when removed from an impression, even with extreme care.

In this situation, crime scene investigators often use products similar to that used by dentists. These dental composition type materials are formed when two different chemicals are mixed together. When mixed, a puttylike substance is produced. This can be pressed or poured into small dents in any hard material such as metals and wood. When left, it hardens and can be removed as a cast, showing quite fine detail. Some of these compounds are hardened by exposure to ultraviolet light rather than heat, which may be a big advantage in a soft or fragile situation.

The disadvantage of these materials is that they are very expensive. Hence, they are used only when the information that could be revealed is very important to a case. Today, most crime scene investigators use a type of silicone plastic mix. When mixed, a very thick liquid paste is produced. If it is to be used to cast an impression on a vertical surface, then a mold is made out of modeling clay. This is pushed into the surface below the mark, and then the plastic mixture is poured into the mold and allowed to set. The result is a flexible, soft plasticlike cast that shows up remarkably small details such as scratch marks made by a hard instrument. A less expensive alternative is epoxy putty, which can be purchased at most hardware stores.

Two Pot Mixtures

Silicone plastic mixes and epoxy putty belong to a family of products that require two separate parts to be mixed together at the time of use. These are known as *two pot mixtures*. The mixing of the two substances causes a chemical reaction between one substance, called casting material, and another, the hardener. The product is a new chemical that is hard but has exactly the same shape and details the original mixture had. Other examples of two pot mixtures include resin and hardener, which mix to form the finish for fiberglass products, and some glues.

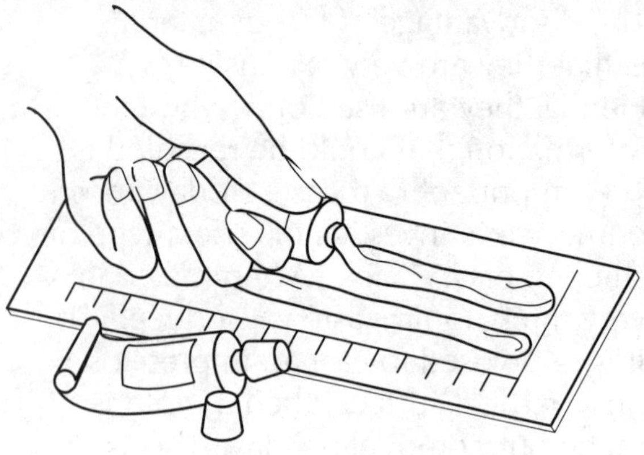

The two pot system: two parts are laid out and then mixed.

When a CSI finds a tool mark that needs to have a permanent record made of it, the plastic mixture has to be prepared in exactly the correct proportion of casting material and hardener. This is done by squeezing out equal lengths of each substance onto a hard plastic sheet. The kit contains two tubes that have openings designed to measure out the exact proportions of each substance required. This ensures accuracy and saves time. The examiner does not have to worry about carefully calculating the proportion of each chemical needed every time a cast is made. The two substances are then thoroughly mixed with a spatula and the paste is scraped into the mold. With practice, the CSI can produce the amount of mixture required to fill the impression very quickly.

Epoxy putty comes in various forms, but generally consists of two materials packaged together in a roll but not yet mixed. A small amount of the putty can be cut off and kneaded in the fingers to mix the two chemicals. When it feels warm to the touch, it indicates that a chemical reaction is taking place as the two components begin to set and harden. It is now ready to use. It must be used immediately as it sets quickly.

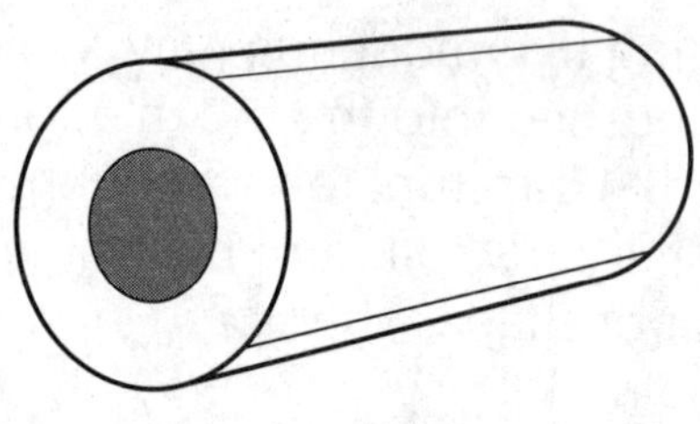

The hardener in the center is completely surrounded by the filler.

© Shell Education

Two Pot Mixtures (cont.)

Comprehension Questions

1. What problems are presented by impressions that are not on a horizontal surface? Explain how these problems are overcome.
2. When is a modeling claylike casting material most useful?
3. What are the advantages and disadvantages of using dental composition to make a cast?
4. When would an epoxy putty product be chosen instead of dental composition in casting a tool mark?

Name ____________________

Two Pot Casting

Materials

- screwdriver, pliers, or other tool to make an impression in lead
- lead sinker or other lead item
- small slice of epoxy putty

Procedure

1. Using a screwdriver or pliers, make a shallow dent or scrape in a piece of lead.

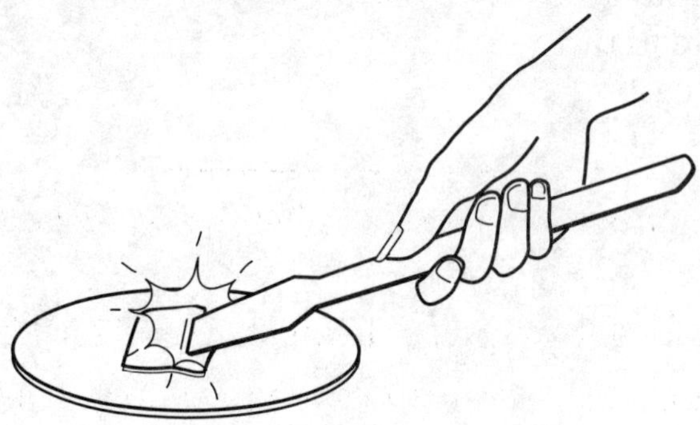

2. Take a small slice of the putty about the thickness of a quarter and knead it according to the directions on the package.

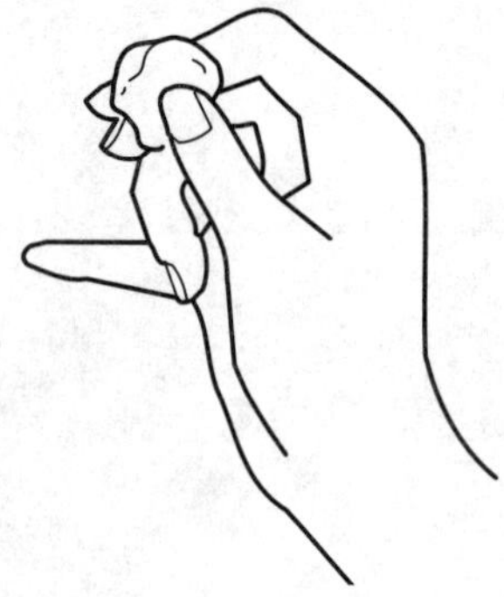

3. Push putty firmly into the impression and leave to set.

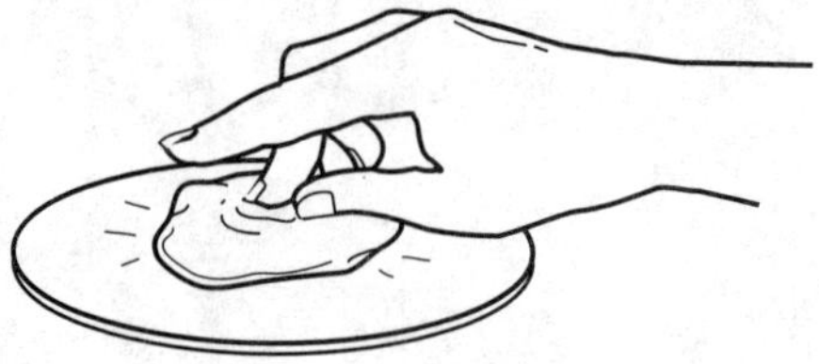

Name ____________________

Two Pot Casting (cont.)

Procedure (cont.)

4. Carefully remove the hardened mold from the impression.

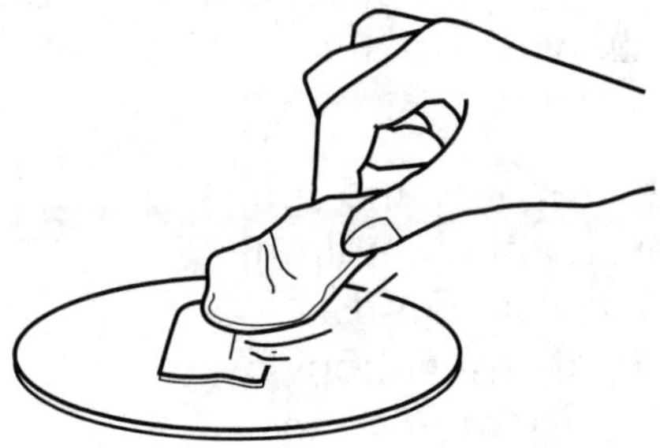

Analysis

1. Record your observations: initial appearance, cast quality, ease of use, value to police, etc.
2. Explain how you prepared the mixture and how it changed on mixing.
3. When pressed into the impression, how long did the mixture take to set?
4. Under what circumstances would a CSI use this type of material at a crime scene?
5. What problems did you find with its use and the cast it produced?

Tooth Marks

Teeth have never been used to identify a person to the same extent as fingerprints or DNA profiling because dental prints change with time. Over the years, teeth become worn down or may be lost to disease or decay. They can move naturally to fill gaps, or they can move from the pulling action of braces. Fillings and dentures will also alter a dental print.

Nevertheless, dental records and prints have often been invaluable in helping to prove identity. Forensic dentists can assist in criminal investigations by studying teeth and teeth impressions. About 80 percent of the time, teeth impressions are used to identify unknown victims. Teeth are one of the hardest substances in the human body, resistant to fire and decomposition, so they are frequently well preserved. Dental X-rays or records showing the exact position of teeth and any fillings can help forensic dentists to match a set of teeth to an individual.

Dental records have also been used to catch criminals. A peckish burglar once took a bite from a piece of cheese at a crime scene and left behind valuable dental evidence for the investigators. Another with an unusually shaped jaw bit into an apple before discarding it at a crime scene. When hard foods are bitten into, the remaining piece of food retains a print of the teeth that bit into it. If a dental print is found in some food, the investigator must record the teeth marks quickly, or preserve the foods, because most foods will shrink and change shape if allowed to dry out. If photographs and casts of the teeth marks are compared to a suspect's dental print, a match between them may prove the burglar's guilt, or at least link the suspect to the evidence.

The human teeth patterns shown here are a textbook set. In reality most people have variations on these, which makes each set unique. The human teeth pattern reflects the diet of an omnivore. Human teeth are designed to both cut and grind a wide variety of foods, including meat, vegetables, and nuts. The incisors at the front do the cutting, the two pointed canine teeth do the ripping, and the molars at the back do the grinding.

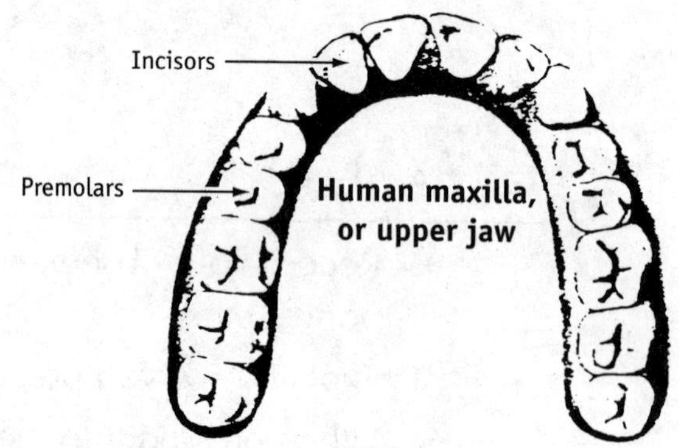

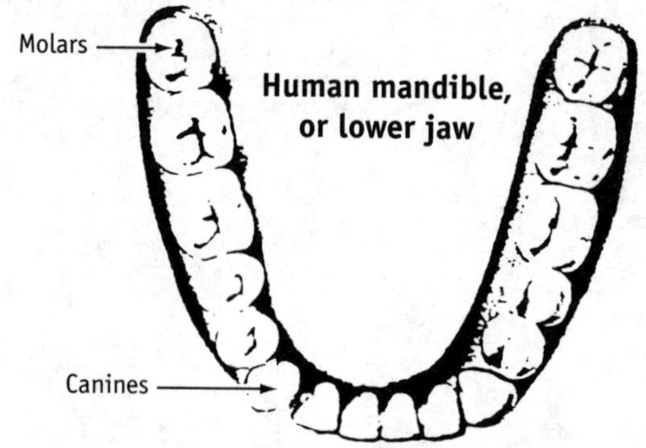

© Shell Education

Tooth Marks (cont.)

Animal Teeth Patterns

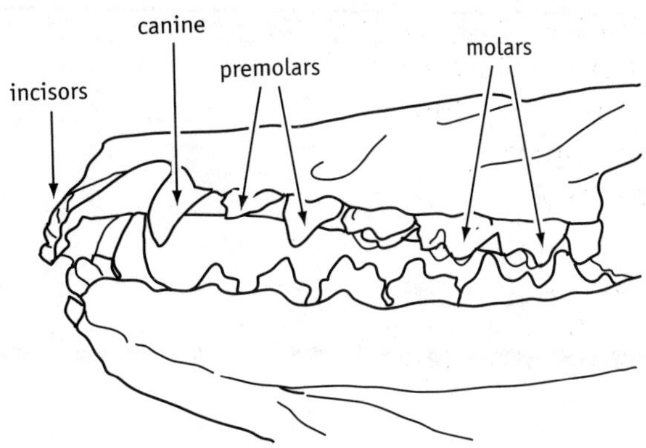

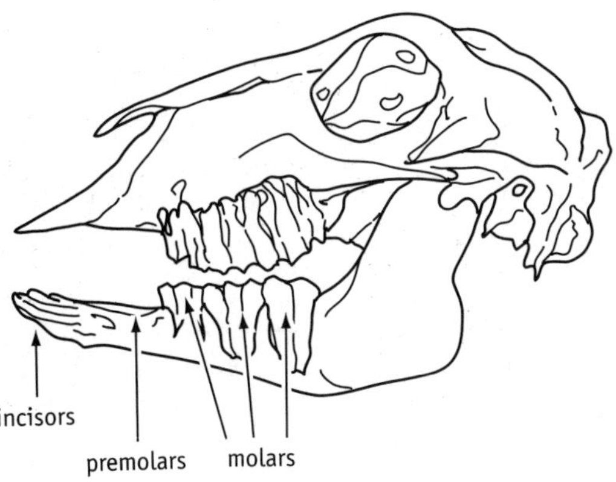

A knowledge of teeth patterns in animals, particularly domestic pets, can also link a suspect to a crime scene. A burglar may be bitten by the family dog while sneaking across the back garden, or bitten by the frightened and cornered family cat while rummaging through a bedroom cupboard.

An animal's teeth prints can also be distinctive for the same reasons as humans: decay, wear, defect, and disease. A pair of domestic dogs of the same breed, age, and health can have markedly different teeth prints simply from years of being fed a different diet by their owners. One could be fed on softer dog biscuits while the other regularly chews on bones and solid meat pieces.

Tooth Marks (cont.)

Comprehension Questions

1. Why are teeth impressions useful in helping to solve a crime?
2. How do the teeth of the upper jaw (maxilla) differ from those of the lower jaw (mandible) in a human?
3. How could dental prints be useful at a crime scene? List all the uses of dental records in Forensic Science.
4. Why should dental prints found in food eaten by a suspect be taken quickly?
5. How does a carnivore's teeth pattern make it more suitable for eating meat rather than plants?
6. When Joe Green came home from work he found that he had been burgled. There was evidence (some denim cotton threads found between his dog's teeth) that the burglar may have been bitten by Joe's dog. When a suspect was found who had some suspicious puncture marks on his thigh (illustration at right), he claimed that they were caused by a bite from his pet rabbit.

   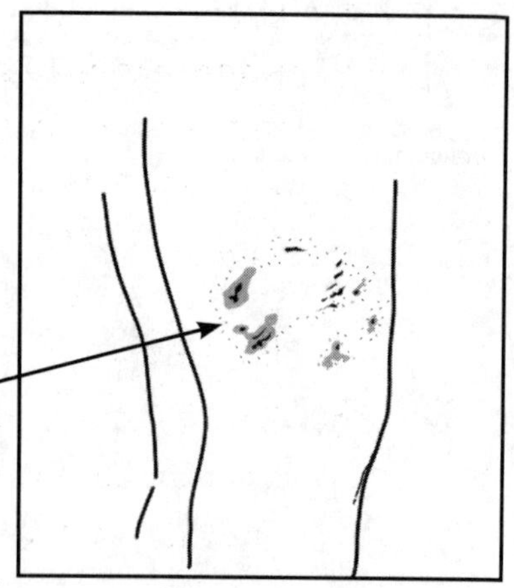

   Explain why the investigator did not believe the suspect. What tests do you think the investigator should carry out to disprove the suspect's story?

 © Shell Education

Name ______________________

Teeth Impressions in Cheese

This activity using cheese and the following activity using apples can be done in conjunction with each other. In this activity you will compare the teeth marks made in some cheese with some volunteers' teeth.

Materials

- one slice of cheese per student

Procedure

1. Bite a large piece out of your slice of cheese so that as many teeth as possible leave their mark on the remaining piece of cheese.
2. Enjoy eating the piece that was bitten off!
3. Reproduce the teeth impression that you left in the cheese (by tracing or photocopying) onto a piece of paper.
4. Working in groups of three or four, copy the cheese impressions of all the members in your group. Each impression should go on a separate piece of paper with the name of the student it came from on the opposite side. Use a different method for each piece of cheese. Do not damage the original cheese impression.
5. Shuffle your group's copies of impressions together. Try to match impression copies with the members of your group partners. Take notes about what works and what doesn't.

cheese bites

Analysis

1. Were there difficulties in identifying one set of impressions from another within your group? Explain your reasons.
2. How did making a paper copy of the bite, rather than using the original pieces of cheese, help in identifying to whom the bite belonged?
3. How do you think making a cast of the volunteers' teeth would help?

Name ______________________________

Teeth Impressions in Apples

This activity using apples and the preceding one using cheese can be done in conjunction with each other. In this activity you will compare the teeth marks made in an apple with a volunteer's teeth.

Materials

- one apple per student

Procedure

1. Make a large deep bite mark into your apple without removing the piece of apple.
2. Compare your cheese bite from the previous activity to your apple bite. Do the two impressions make it possible to match the apple bite with the cheese bite?
3. If you make a second bite into your apple, but at a different place, are the two teeth marks the same? Would you be able to recognize, without doubt, that both marks were made by the same person biting the apple, or does it look like it may have been shared by two different suspects?
4. Make a drawing of one of the set of teeth marks that you have left in your apple.
5. When you have finished your work you can destroy the evidence: finish eating your apple and cheese!

apple bites

Analysis

1. What is the main feature that separates the look of your impression compared to that of the person sitting next to you?
2. What other differences are there when you compare the two shapes?
3. Have you left any other forensic evidence on the remaining apple core?

Name ________________________________

Comparing Dental Casts

Materials

- 10 dental casts, 5 upper and 5 lower (See local orthodontist or dental technician for casts that are no longer needed. For more interest, try to select unusual teeth profiles.)
- modeling clay

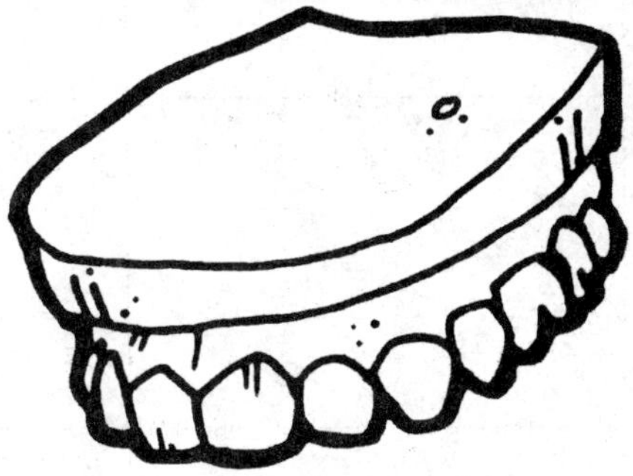

Procedure

1. Observe the dental characteristics of the other members of your group.
2. Write a list of the features common to the teeth of the lower jaw (mandible).
3. Write another list of features common to the teeth of the upper jaw (maxilla).
4. Draw and label simple diagrams to illustrate your answer. Consider shape, size, and angle.
5. On desks around the room, you will find plaster dental casts that have been marked with one of the letters A to J. These are genuine casts that have come from real people.
6. Copy Table 1 (page 138) into your science notebook, and then, using your observations from Step 1 above, decide which of the letters represents a mandible (L) and which represents a maxilla (U). Place a *U* or an *L* in the table next to each letter. Hint: There are five of each. Write notes on characteristics of each cast.

Name ______________________

Comparing Dental Casts (cont.)

Procedure (cont.)

Table 1

Cast	Maxilla or Mandible?	Notes
A		
B		
C		
D		
E		
F		
G		
H		
I		
J		

7. You will now be shown five numbered molds made of clay. They have each had the bite from a set of the plaster casts impressed in them. You will notice that each contains the imprint of an upper (maxilla) and a lower (mandible).
8. Copy Table 2 into your science notebook and then record the number of the cast that was impressed in the clay.

Table 2

Cast	1	2	3	4	5
maxilla					
mandible					

 © Shell Education

Name ______________________________

Comparing Dental Casts (cont.)

Analysis

1. What are the advantages of each method (the plastercast and the modeling clay impression) to the forensic scientist?
2. What are the disadvantages of each method to the forensic scientist?
3. Was it relatively easy to distinguish among the different sets of teeth casts? Why?
4. Do you think a jury would be more convinced with matching a plaster cast or a photograph as evidence? Why?
5. Were there any features of all the casts that tended to be similar in most cases? If so, what were they?

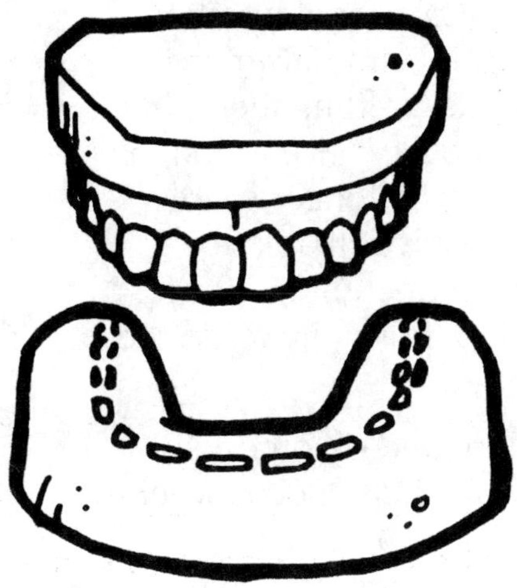

dental cast impression in modeling clay

Chromatography

Forgery is the changing of a document, or the making of an imitation of something, with the intent to break the law.

Large-scope forgery consists of creating fake goods and selling them under a trusted brand name. Companies with famous brand names put a lot of money into research and development of their product. Their products are usually fairly expensive and of good quality. Industrial forgers copy products, often using poorer quality and cheaper materials, so that they can be sold very cheaply.

Alternately, many stolen goods—such as cars, bikes, keys, tools, and guns—carry identification marks or serial numbers imprinted on them. Criminals try to remove these marks by filing them, in order to avoid discovery. Even though these marks may be no longer visible, the forensic scientist is still able to restore them. In an upcoming activity, you will have the opportunity to do the same.

The most common kind of forgery is personal forgery. This can occur when someone writes a signature that is not their own or alters a figure or some words. Common examples are forging signatures or altering the amounts on checks, wills, and insurance documents.

Checks may be forged by blotting out words or numbers and replacing them with other words or numbers. A forgery may also add extra words or numbers to ones already there—for example, *six* can be changed to *sixty* and $6 to $60. This type of forgery can be detected if it can be shown that different inks have been used on different parts of the check or document.

Chromatography and Forgery

The inks used in pens are made up of a mixture of dyes or pigments. If these dyes can be separated, it can be seen from which colors the ink is made. The ink from two different pens may seem the same color when on paper, but be made up of different dyes. Chromatography is the method of separating the dyes.

It works like this: When a strip of absorbent paper is hung with one end in a beaker of water, the water will soak up into the paper. If an ink mark that is soluble in water is above the water surface, then as the water passes through the ink mark, some dyes in the ink mixture are attracted to the water and travel up the paper. The distance the pigment travels depends on the type of solvent used and the weight and size of the dye molecules. The resulting pattern of colors is called a chromatogram.

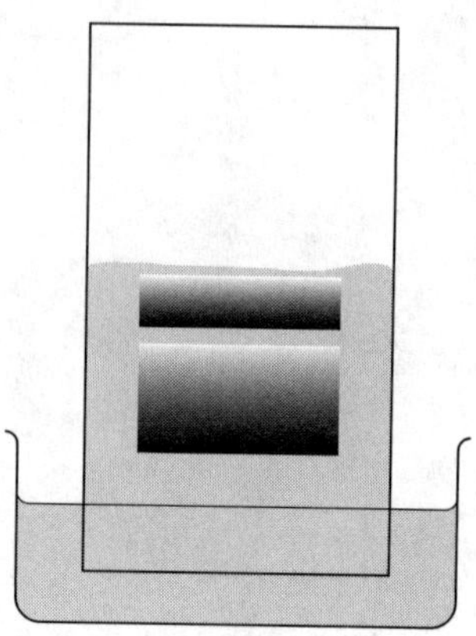

© Shell Education

Chromatography (cont.)

Comprehension Questions

1. Give three examples of forgery.
2. What negative effects can industrial forgery have?
3. Why is altering a check known as personal forgery?
4. What information can be gained from a chromatogram?
5. Describe a possible crime scenario in which a forensic scientist might want to carry out a chromatography test.

Name ______________________

Comparing Pens

The police need assistance in determining who might have written a ransom note left at a crime scene. The ransom note was written on white blotting paper with a black felt pen. A number of suspects have been identified and their pens seized. You need to figure out which one of the pens, if any, was used to write the ransom note.

Materials

- part of the ransom note
- numbered suspects' black felt pens
- strips of filter or chromatography paper
- large container or trough of water
- pencil or stick to hold the strips of paper

Procedure

1. Using one felt pen, draw a line on the paper strip 2 cm above the bottom of the paper. Label your paper strip in pencil at the top of the strip.

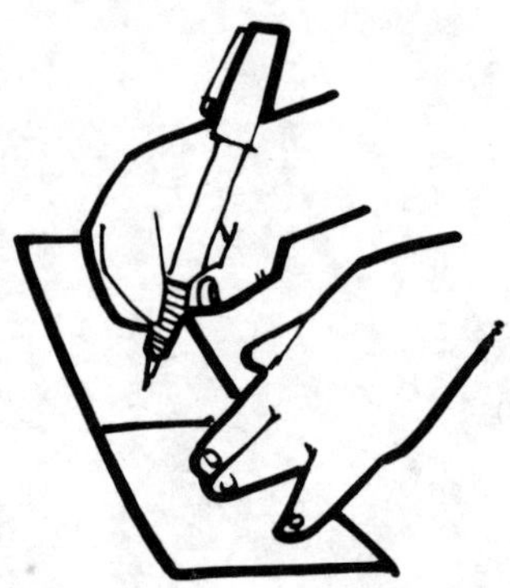

2. Attach your filter paper strip to the pencil or stick.

3. Repeat Steps 1 and 2 with the other papers marked with the suspects' black felt pens and also a sample of the ransom note.

Name ______________________________

Comparing Pens (cont.)

Procedure (cont.)

4. Lay the pencils with the paper strips across the container of water so that all the strips are hanging with the ink marks above the water surface.

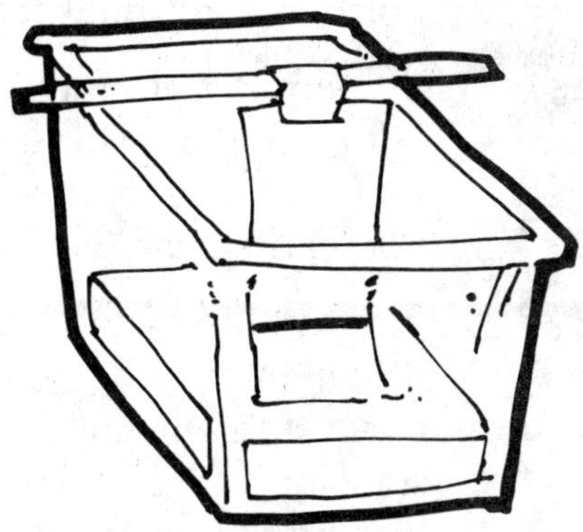

5. Leave for 10 minutes or until the water has traveled about halfway up the strip, carrying the dyes with it. Remove and compare the color patterns.

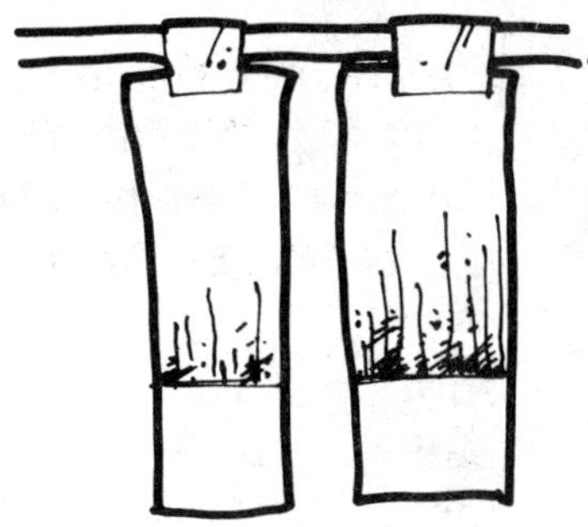

Analysis

1. Which pen contained the greatest number of dyes?
2. Why did some dyes travel farther than others?
3. Were there any inks that did not travel up the paper, or separate into other colors? If so, which ones, and why do you think this ink did not soak up with the water?
4. Which chromatograph was closest to the one from the ransom note?
5. What could you conclude about the pen that drew the line with a chromatograph closest to the ransom note?
6. Why should the ink on the filter paper be above the water level?
7. Why were you asked to label your paper strip in pencil and at the top of the paper?
8. If the suspect's pen had not contained water-soluble ink, water could not have been used. What other solvents may be used in chromatography?

Metal Forgery

Metals are made up of tiny particles called atoms that are arranged in a regular and orderly pattern (figure A).

If a number is stamped on the metal, the layers of atoms below the mark are compressed (squashed) (figure B).

If the marks are filed away, the atoms left behind are still squashed where the mark was made; however, from above, you cannot see the difference.

If a solution called Fry's reagent is used, it will change the appearance of the parts of the metal where the atoms are squashed. This will reveal the mark that was filed away (figure C).

Fry's reagent is a corrosive acid that reacts with the atoms in the metal. In the area where the metal was punched, the atoms are closer together and so react with the acid faster than the surrounding area. Hence, an etched pattern, showing a clear outline of the original marks, will appear. Fry's reagent is so corrosive that it must only be used by qualified science staff in a science lab. It should only be demonstrated and not done by students.

The drawing on the right shows a registration mark stamped into a bicycle. Thieves may try to file the impression away and repaint the bike. Removal of the paint and treatment with a suitable etching reagent will show the number that has been filed away.

figure A

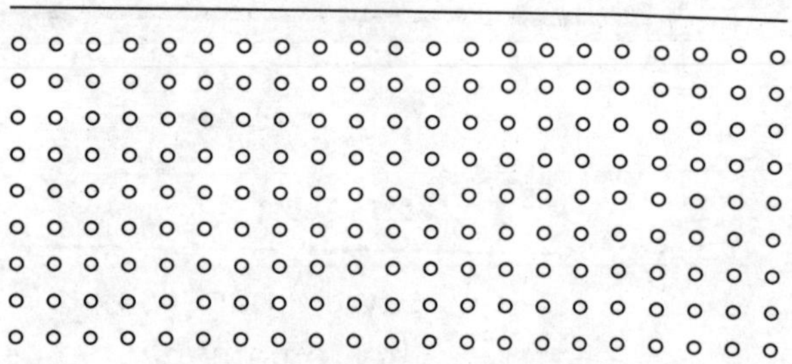

figure B

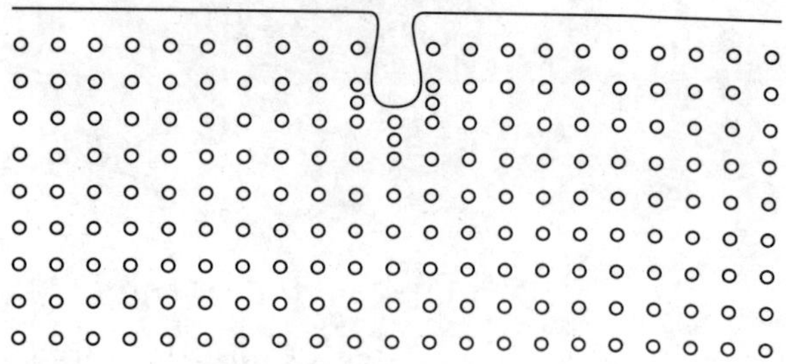

figure C

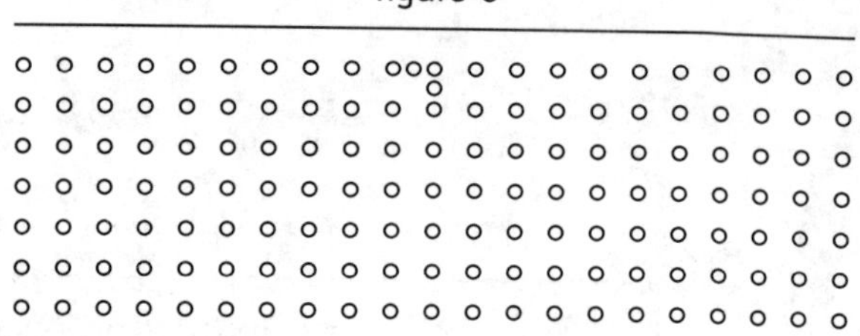

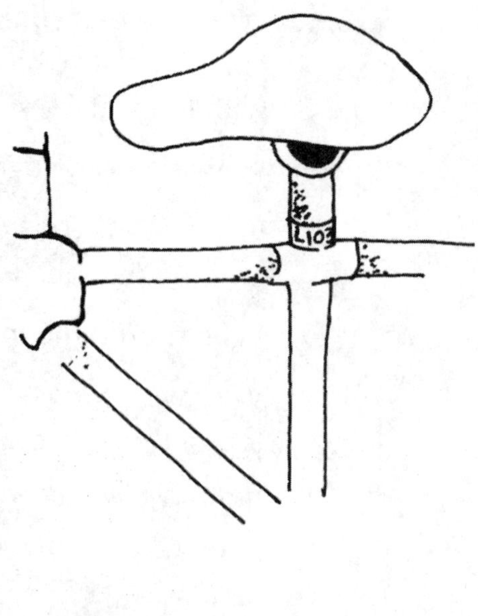

© Shell Education

Metal Forgery (cont.)

Comprehension Questions

1. How can permanent numbers be attached to a bike or car engine?
2. Describe how a dishonest person removes such numbers.
3. Why is it so difficult to remove numbers completely from metals?
4. What effect does Fry's reagent have on a metal?
5. Why should the use of Fry's reagent only be demonstrated by qualified staff?

Name ______________________________

Uncovering Metal Forgery

The solutions used in this experiment are very corrosive and should not be handled without gloves.

Materials

- sample of metal (mild steel) that has had a punched mark removed by filing
- gloves
- safety glasses
- metal tongs
- cotton wool
- beaker of diluted ammonia large enough to hold the metal
- Bunsen burner
- nitric acid (20%)
- acetone
- Fry's reagent (copper chloride and hydrochloric acid solution)

Procedure

1. Wearing gloves and safety glasses, and using tongs, dip some cotton wool in acetone and clean any grease from the metal.

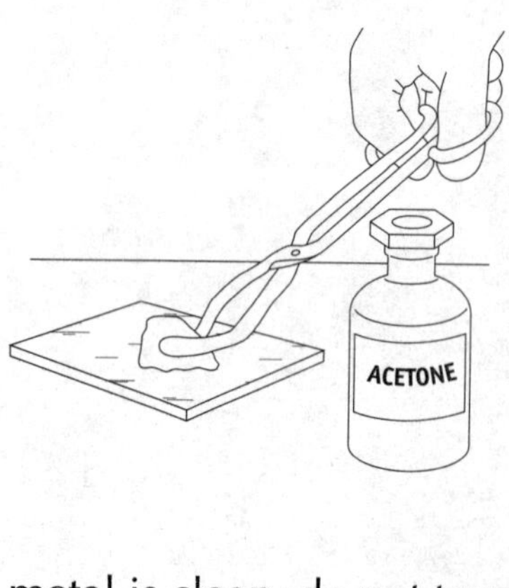

2. When the metal is clean, do not touch it again with your fingers.

 © Shell Education

Name ____________________

Uncovering Metal Forgery (cont.)

Procedure (cont.)

3. Using the tongs, gently heat the metal in a low flame for a few seconds. Do not let the metal glow red hot.

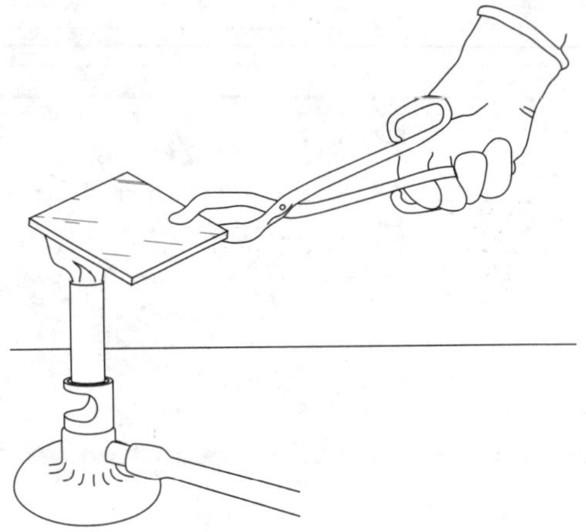

4. Leave the metal to cool, then rub it for one minute with cotton wool dipped in Fry's reagent. Take care not to get any on you.

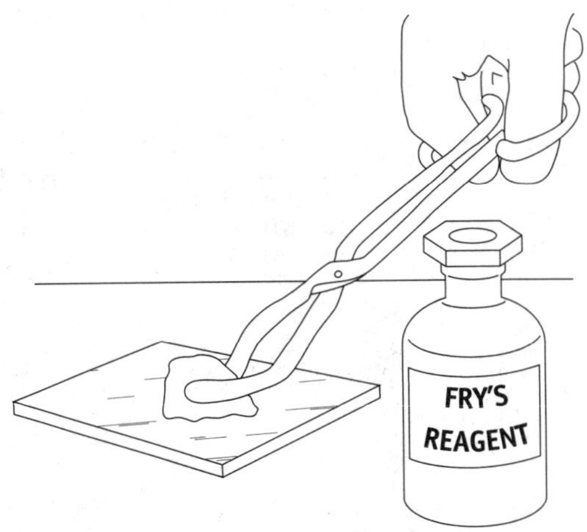

5. Dry the metal with clean cotton wool. Using tongs, dip a piece of clean cotton wool into nitric acid and rub the metal for one minute.

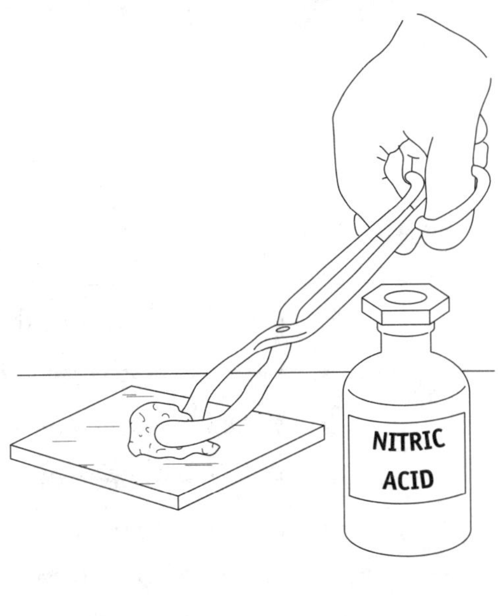

Name ____________________

Uncovering Metal Forgery (cont.)

Procedure (cont.)

6. Dry the metal again with clean cotton wool.

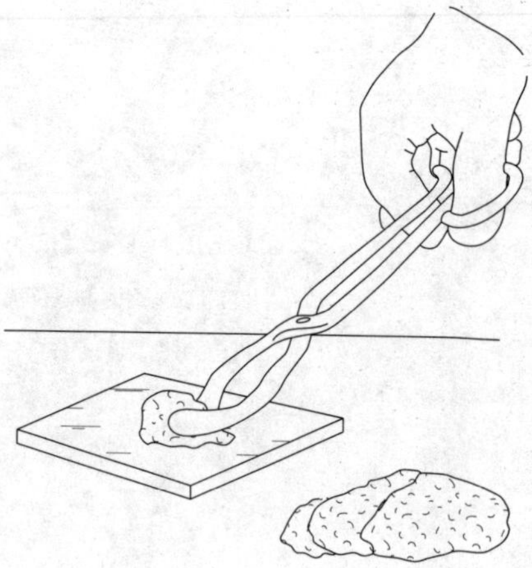

7. Repeat steps 4 to 6 until the forgery becomes clear.

8. Using tongs, wash the metal in ammonia in a beaker. Dry the metal with clean cotton wool.

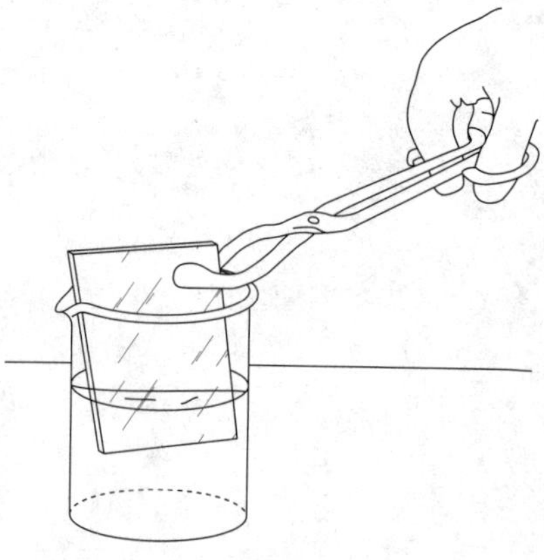

Analysis

1. Draw a picture of the marks found on the piece of metal.
2. Why is mild steel suggested as a suitable metal for this practical exercise?
3. Why are gloves as well as tongs used in this exercise?
4. What is the reason for not touching the metal with your hands in step 2?
5. Give some examples of forgeries where numbers might be filed off metal and replaced with new ones.

 © Shell Education

Handwriting

Handwriting experts are called in most often when a signature is believed to be forged. They are also called in when two samples of handwriting must be compared to check that the same person wrote them.

The fundamental principle common to all document examination involves a comparison of the suspect or disputed document with a known specimen of a person's signature or handwriting.

An individual's handwriting is personal and depends for its character on the interaction of the brain, eye, and hand. It is affected by the person's physical and emotional state, the position in which they are writing, and other circumstances—such as the type of pen or pencil—that may control the speed. A person may have several handwriting styles and several signatures. On the other hand, two identical signatures could look suspiciously like a photocopy or good-quality tracing.

When comparing two samples of handwriting, a handwriting expert would particularly look at:

- the pattern of how high and how low the letters go
- the average space between the words or some letters
- the pressure and fluency of the writing
- the slope of the writing (it can be backhand [\] or normal [/] or upright [|])
- the relationship of the letters with the horizontal line
- the general style of writing (cursive, printing, or block letters)
- the style of writing certain letters—for example:

S or s, t or t, r or r,
f or f, b or b, p or p

An expert in analyzing handwriting can generally tell if a person is right-handed and pulls the pen across the page, or left-handed and pushes the pen across the page.

A right-handed person pulls the pen so that it follows the wrist, while a left-handed person pushes the pen ahead of the wrist. These two very different actions put different emphasis on the down and up strokes in letter formation, even if the actual shape of each letter is very similar.

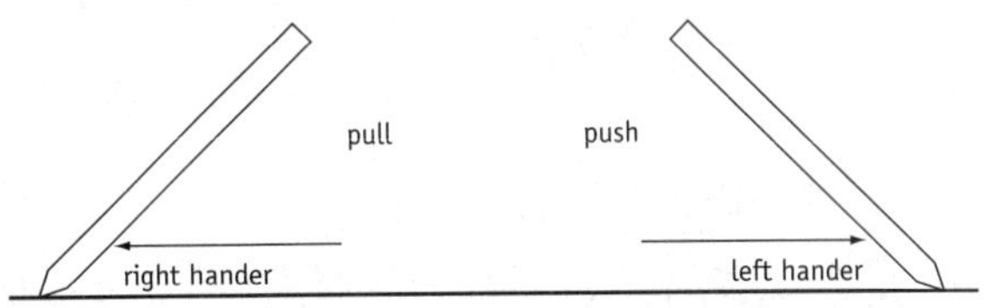

Spaces Comparison

A sheet of tracing paper can be placed over the signature and a dot drawn at the end of any letter that is not joined to the next one. This includes spaces between letters as well as between words. The pattern shows where the pen of the writer was taken off the page. The gaps a person leaves are also usually very distinctive.

Handwriting (cont.)

Top-of-Letter Comparison

Another sheet of tracing paper is placed over a suspect signature, and a small dot is drawn on the highest point or points of each letter as shown below. When the tracing paper is removed, the dots are joined to form a zigzag line. This can then be compared to the pattern formed from the genuine or known, signature.

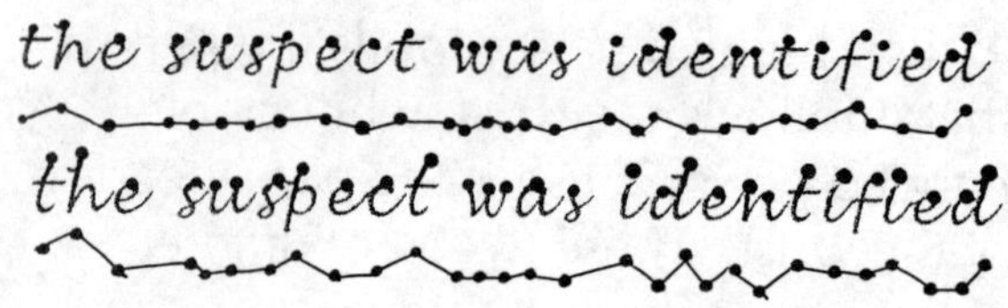

While a casual observation of the letters themselves can detect no obvious differences, the two line graphs formed by the "top-of-letter" technique show several clear differences.

Bottom-of-Letter Comparison

This is similar to the previous technique but, as the name suggests, a dot is placed on the lowest point or points of each letter. Again, the two zigzag patterns of the known and suspect writing can be compared.

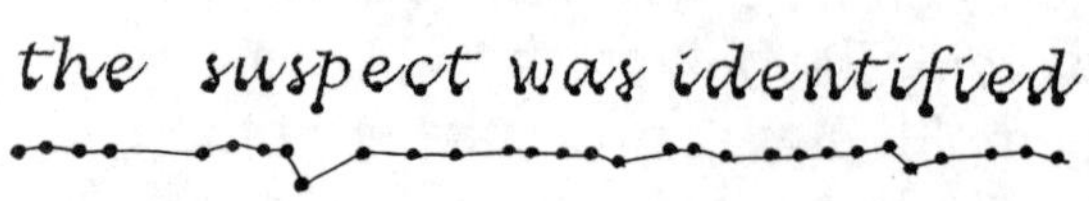

Slope Comparison

For this technique, a line is drawn on the tracing paper, indicating each letter's slope. This, too, is a very individual characteristic.

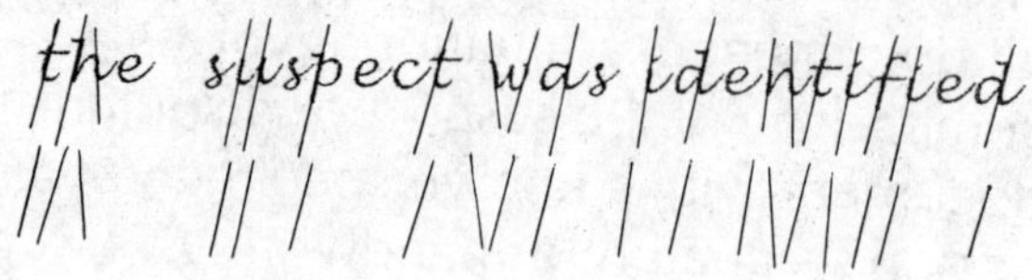

© Shell Education

Comprehension Questions

1. Describe two types of situations in which a handwriting expert might be called in.
2. List seven things that a handwriting expert might look for when comparing two samples of handwriting.
3. What information about the writer can a handwriting expert gain from one sample?
4. Describe three different methods of comparison an expert might use in comparing handwriting.
5. How could these comparisons be done?

Name ______________________________

Comparing Handwriting

On Thursday, September 28, businesswoman Ms. Cynthia Shande was found on the floor of her upstairs hall. She had been poisoned, and foul play was suspected. She was found clutching a handwritten will leaving all her possessions to her cook, Mrs. Muriel Thornton.

Ms. Shande's nephew accused Mrs. Thornton of forging the will and of murdering his unmarried aunt for her possessions. The police were brought in.

You are a police forensic scientist specializing in disputed documents and handwriting, and you must compare the handwriting that has been found in Ms. Shande's diary with that on the will.

Wednesday 27th September
Several times today I did not
feel well. In the office it was
decided that rather than
persevere.

extract from diary

27 September, Wednesday
I hereby beq ueath all my
worldly goods to my cook Mrs
Muriel Thornton. For several
years she has done a good job
of looking after me.

extract from will

Materials

- tracing paper
- pencil

 © Shell Education

Name ______________________________

Comparing Handwriting (cont.)

Procedure

1. Draw a table as shown below, and complete the comparisons listed.

Feature Compared	From Diary	From Will
slope of writing		
shape of letter *s*		
average gap between words		
top-of-letter comparison		

Analysis

1. Do you think that both samples of writing were written by Ms. Shande? Explain in detail all the differences or similarities that have led you to make this conclusion.
2. What other information would be helpful in solving this crime?
3. In pairs, write two sentences each, then swap with the other person and try to copy their writing. How easy is it to copy someone else's handwriting?

Typewriters

Before personal computers became so common, typewriters were used extensively. Formal and legal documents were either handwritten or typed. A criminal might have used a typewriter to write a threatening letter or ransom note in order to avoid his or her handwriting being recognized.

A forensic expert was often able to match a sample of typescript to a particular typewriter brand or model. They could vary in where the center point of *M* or *W* was or where the crossbars were on *f* or *t*.

As a typewriter became older, some letters would show wear in particular places. These errors would show up consistently every time the letter was typed throughout the whole document. Wear on these mechanical preelectronic machines was another factor that created distinctions between them. Levers, springs, cogs, and metal parts hitting and rubbing on each other all contributed to uneven wear and therefore a uniqueness in typing quality. This made many typewriters distinctive and, therefore, traceable. This meant that it could be quite easy to match a document with the exact typewriter on which it was written and hence eventually determine who wrote it.

The range in ink types was much larger than is now available for computers. There were greater numbers of manufacturers and supplier networks. Inks did not just come from a few global suppliers, but from many local sources, and each of these again had their own brand range and formulae. This made tracing easier because each ink was more distinctive.

In 1924, a 14-year-old boy was kidnapped and found murdered before any ransom money could be paid. An unusual pair of glasses was found at the site where the body was located and this led to one person whose alibi was very shaky—Nathan Leopold, a rich and brilliant 19-year-old student. Police also questioned Leopold's close friend and fellow student, 18-year-old Richard Loeb. They both became prime suspects.

When a witness came forward, claiming to have seen two men dumping a typewriter in a local lagoon, an immediate search was made and the lagoon dragged. A typewriting machine was found and sent to the laboratory for forensic analysis. By then, the police had matched the type on the ransom letters with the type on some of Richard Loeb's student essays. It was soon confirmed that the dumped typewriter was the machine on which both the ransom notes and Loeb's essays had been typed.

Both young men were found guilty of murder and kidnapping and were sentenced to life imprisonment.

© Shell Education

Typewriters (cont.)

Comprehension Questions

1. The piece of typewriter ribbon below was recovered from a suspect's rubbish bin. The partly destroyed message is a mirror image of what had been typed on to it. Can you work out what the message says exactly? (Hint: Do you have a mirror handy?)

2. What do you think the writer of this message might have been trying to accomplish?

3. Why would this piece of evidence not have existed if the suspect had used a computer?

4. Why are ransom notes produced on typewriters easier to trace than those done on computers?

Indentations

A blackmail letter, or a threatening message on notepaper, may be the key to solving a crime. This may still be possible even if the actual document is not available to the police.

If the writing is on a special type of paper—such as recycled, wood-free, or coated—it is possible to match it to paper from the same batch at a suspect's house or office. It may bear a unique watermark that can indicate where the paper was made or bought.

A note may have been torn from a page, or torn roughly into pieces so that the message could not be read again. Under a microscope, the edges can be matched up, the pieces fitted together, and the message revealed. An electron microscope can be used if even closer analysis is required.

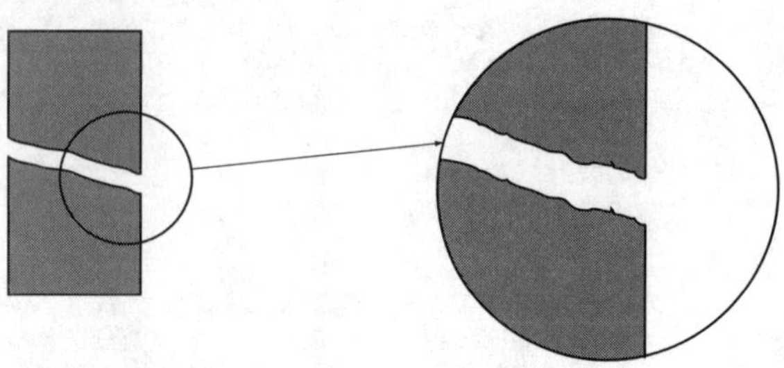

Many people press quite heavily when they write, especially when using a ballpoint pen. Such writing can leave indentations on any sheets underneath the paper being written on. The print can often be seen by allowing light to fall on it at an angle. By holding the paper at an angle near the light source, it is often quite easy to see these indentations. They can be photographed for a permanent record. Gentle rubbing with a soft pencil or some powder may also reveal the indentations by coloring the surface but leaving the indented parts uncolored.

The figure below shows how a criminal writing heavily on a notepad has left evidence of a message on the underlying sheet of paper for anyone to find.

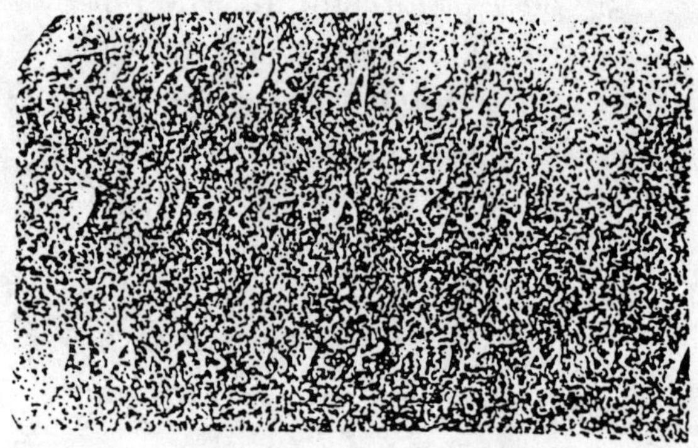

The photograph was made by placing the flash at the side so that one side of the edges of the impressions cast a shadow, while the opposite edge is lit up brightly. This allows the message to be read more easily. It can also be used as a permanent record if the case should go to trial.

© Shell Education

Indentations (cont.)

Electrostatic Imaging to Reveal Indentations

Forensic scientists can also employ electrostatic imaging to uncover indentations on paper. First, the suspect document is placed face upwards on the vacuum bed of the machine and covered with a thin transparent film. The film is pulled against the document by a vacuum pump.

The indentations are then electrically charged before being covered with a fine powder of inked beads that attach to the indentations. They can be photographed or kept in place with adhesive film. The original document remains unmarked, which is important in case further tests need to be carried out.

The figures below are photographs of the same document. They are both impressions of a page that was below a sheet that had been written on with a pen.

The first figure shows the page photographed under oblique light. The second figure is the same page, but it has been processed using an electrostatic imaging system. This provides the forensic scientist with more detail than the photograph.

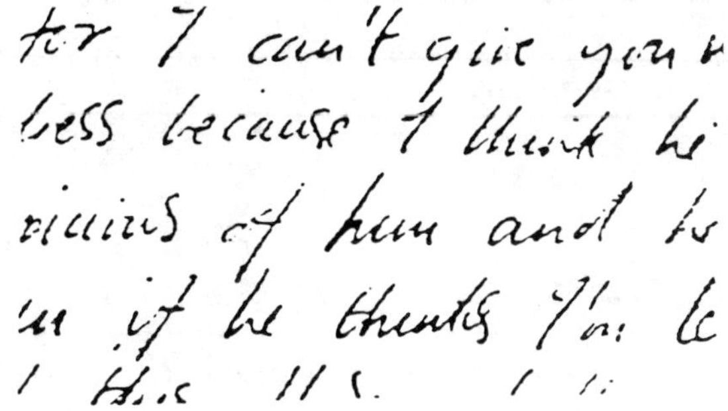

Comprehension Questions

1. Explain how indented writing is produced.
2. What are two simple ways in which indented writing can be made visible?
3. How does electrostatic imaging work?
4. Give two reasons why electrostatic imaging is better than the ways mentioned in question 2.
5. Why is a photograph usually taken of the revealed message?
6. Write a short paragraph that describes how matching torn paper can be crucial evidence.

Name ____________________

Reading Indentations

In this activity you are going to make your own indentations and then try to read someone else's message by shading the top surface.

Materials

- sharp pencil and other writing instruments
- an assortment of paper types, each type with several pieces
- soft "B" lead pencil or similar colored pencil

Procedure

1. With some layers of paper resting on a soft surface, write a message with a sharp pencil. You may like to try several messages, each time pressing with different amounts of force. Try resting the papers on different surfaces.
2. Remove the top sheet that you wrote on and dispose of it. Now inspect the sheet below. With the light coming from the side, can you read the writing?
3. Swap your message with a friend and see if you can read each other's notes. Very gently rub some pencil over the indentations. This should reveal the message. Stick a sample in your science notebook.

4. Repeat this exercise, using a few different writing instruments and different types of paper.

 © Shell Education

Name ____________________

Reading Indentations (cont.)

Procedure (cont.)

5. Repeat this exercise again, but this time use the same pen on different paper types.

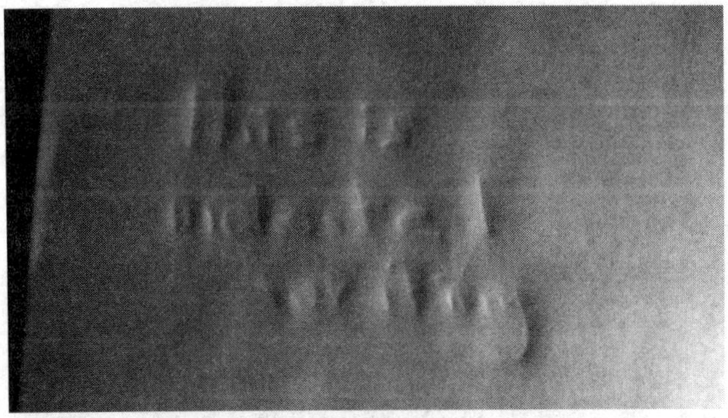

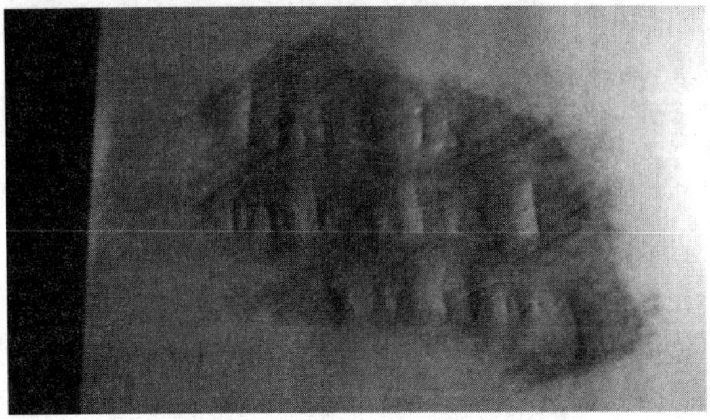

Analysis

1. How clearly could you read the messages?
2. What sort of things changed the clarity of the indentations?
3. Did you try resting the pages on both hard and soft surfaces? Which type of surface caused the clearest indentations?
4. How did the type of pen that you used affect the impressions?
5. How did the type of paper that you used affect the impressions?
6. Write a paragraph describing a crime scene in which indented writing was used as the main evidence to solve it.

Seat Belts

It is not speed that kills or injures people, but the force of an impact on their bodies when they collide with a stationary object. The greater the speed, the greater the force of the impact, and so the more dangerous it is for the person.

Many jurisdictions have laws that make not wearing a seat belt illegal. Before seat belt wearing was made compulsory, extensive studies were done comparing the injuries sustained in accidents by drivers who were wearing seat belts and those who were not. The table below shows the results of one such study.

A survey of 20,000 drivers who were involved in car accidents was conducted to see how the wearing of seat belts affected the type of injuries that were sustained.

Type of Injury	Unbelted Drivers	Belted Drivers
Fatal	17	3
Serious	121	75
Slight	387	254
No injury	9,475	9,668
Total	10,000	10,000

Seatbelt webbing is made from special polyesters that must conform to very strict standards that include strength and the ability to both stretch under a load and then recover from the stretch. It must also be resistant to sunlight degradation and abrasion. Tests are carried out to ensure that all seatbelt webbing meets these standards.

Comprehension Questions

1. Imagine you are in charge of making a decision regarding the wearing of seatbelts. Using the figures in the table, what decision would you make? Give reasons for your decision.

2. People who are caught not wearing seat belts can be fined, and the driver's right to drive may be taken away. Discuss how fair you think this is. If you disagree with this punishment, suggest what you would do if you were in charge and give reasons for your answer.

3. Are there any people who are exempt from wearing a seat belt where you live? Find out what the laws are regarding the wearing of seat belts for pregnant mothers, small toddlers, and very young babies.

4. When do seat belts suffer abrasion? What damage can sunlight do to seatbelt webbing? Explain why seatbelt webbing must be resistant to both abrasion and damage from sunlight.

5. Describe how a standards laboratory might test the strength of the fibers in seatbelt webbing. What mass do you think it should be able to hold?

6. Some argue that it is our democratic right to decide for ourselves whether to wear a seat belt or risk injury. Do you agree? Why or why not?

© Shell Education

Inertia

The reason why a person keeps moving forward in a collision is the property of *inertia*. It means that a body will continue moving in the direction it was going or will remain at rest, unless it is acted on by a force. This is also called Newton's First Law of Motion.

This property is clearly seen if you are standing up in a stationary bus. If the bus takes off suddenly, your feet, which are attached to the bus floor, will move forward with the bus because this force is acting on your feet. However, the rest of your body will try to remain behind where you were and you might feel as if you were falling backwards.

Now if the bus stops suddenly, your feet, which are in contact with the bus floor, will stop, but the rest of your body will attempt to continue moving forward at the same speed until your legs, which are attached to your feet, pull your body back. This means that you might feel as if you were falling forwards.

Comprehension Questions

1. Why do you think all new cars now have headrests above the actual seats? Explain how they should be adjusted and why.
2. Explain how whiplash injuries might occur. What can be done to avoid these injuries?
3. Discuss why station wagon owners who carry heavy loads in the backs of their cars are advised to have a strong grill between the back section and passenger compartment.
4. Some magicians are able to do a trick in which they give a tablecloth a very quick tug such that the tablecloth is pulled out from under the dishes, which are left standing in their original places on the table. Use the concept of inertia to explain how this is done.
5. Describe, using the word *inertia*, what happens when a passenger not wearing a seat belt is in a car that collides with a tree. Explain the difference when the passenger is wearing a seat belt.

Name ______________________

Collision!

In this activity you are going to investigate what happens when a car and passengers are involved in a collision.

Materials

- 2 small toy cars
- 2 modeling clay passengers
- some masking or sticky tape
- a wooden ramp about 1-2 m long
- books, blocks, or bricks
- a 40 cm or 1 meter ruler

Procedure

1. Create a table of results in your science notebook, as shown below. Record the distance and direction in which passengers are thrown.

Test	Ramp Height	Run 1	Run 2	Run 3	Average
slow	30 cm				
fast	40 cm				
slow + tape	30 cm				
fast + tape	40 cm				

© Shell Education

Name ______________________________

Collision! (cont.)

Procedure (cont.)

2. Set up car A with its "passenger" at the top of the ramp, and car B and its "passenger" stationary at the bottom.
3. Release car A and observe what happens to both passengers when the cars collide. Measure and record the distances and directions in which they fell. Repeat three times.
4. Now raise the ramp farther, using a book or brick. This will increase the speed of the car. Repeat the same steps three times and record your results.
5. Lastly, lower the ramp height back to the original height, but this time use masking tape to fix both passengers to their car. Repeat the collision three times and record your results.

Analysis

1. Explain why each test was carried out three times and then the average calculated.
2. Describe what happened to the average distance the passengers were thrown out when the speed was increased. Did the direction in which they fell change? Speculate why.
3. What do you think the masking tape represented?
4. What happened to the passengers when the masking tape was used?
5. How can the results from this experiment be used to argue that it is safer to wear seat belts?
6. What did you notice about the direction in which each passenger moved after the collision? Explain why this happens.
7. What can you conclude about the seriousness of injuries to passengers when (a) the speed of the vehicles is increased? and (b) seat belts are worn?

Answer Key

Page 12

1. Forensic science is the using of scientific techniques to solve crimes.
2. Solving crimes became a science about 100 years ago. This was influenced a lot by Locard and his work.
3. It is now more difficult for criminals because of modern techniques and a knowledge of what evidence is useful.
4. Eyewitness reports and being caught "red-handed"
5. A good eyewitness is alert and observant, and notes the appearance and car registration numbers of anyone acting suspiciously.
6. This principle means that whenever there is contact between a person and another person or an object, some small particles always move from one to the other, in both directions.
7. A contact trace is the microscopic evidence that is not obvious to the untrained observer. You don't need a microscope to see a knife, but you would if there were any fingerprints on it.
8. Contact traces are important when a criminal has tried to clean up and remove all obvious evidence.

Page 14

1. three
2. one; running
3. two, one male, one female; female driving; male with hat
4. late-model sedan, license plate XYZ 123, dent and broken headlight on driver's side
5. collecting the trash
6. suburban shops and neat houses
7. a van
8. houses in background are one-story, with TV antennae and lawns
9. a dog running ahead of the child
10. boy and dog look hot and sweaty; person riding a bike in background; female driver looks angry/upset; male is smirking; car and postal carrier outside fish and chip shop
11. description of car; license number; color; damage; direction of travel; number of people in car and description; men as witness and to confirm time

Page 15

light switch is down; no lightbulb in lamp; lightbulb wirer is black; star on detective's cap; detective's left wrist goes inside coat sleeve; no buttons on coat cuffs; sign text is backward; detective has black hair; detective has five fingers on left hand; the eyes in the right-hand painting are different; detective's eye is different; larger black buttons on coat

Page 18

1. Check for any danger to self; check any injured people; give first aid; call ambulance; do not touch anything; secure the site; call for police backup; get names of any witnesses.
2. CSI searches the scene; detective in charge organizes everything that needs to be done.
3. CSIs wear special overalls and overshoes, use boardwalks, and approach the scene from the same place as the first police officer or witness did.
4. The investigators need a record of the crime scene that is as accurate as possible. Photos and maps help a court to better understand the crime.
5. A ruler in a photo helps to record the actual size of an object.
6. A forensic pathologist is called to the scene if a body is found. His or her main responsibility is to find the cause and time of death.

Page 19

1. The clothing keeps them from contaminating the scene.
2. This is done so there is no danger of cross-contamination of scenes.
3. This is done so that nothing is lost or contaminated.
4. Where and when the item was found and by whom it was collected.
5. A registered number is added to the label, and the item's movements around the lab are

Answer Key (cont.)

recorded there so that where the item is and with whom are always known.

6. A contaminated item cannot be used as evidence.
7. The time and date

Page 21

1. a. Dental records, age, and condition of teeth to identify a body where fingerprints may not be possible; for example, where a body is burned beyond recognition
   b. May give a "profile" (characteristics) of a type of criminal who might carry out the type of crime that is being investigated
   c. Studies insects, so may be asked to identify larvae or the age of maggots found on a dead body to estimate the time of death
   d. Studies body fluids, and may give an opinion on diseases, drugs, or other chemicals in a victim's blood
   e. Will inspect a dead body and do the postmortem to confirm the cause of death
2. A forensic scientist is an expert employed full-time to help solve crimes. An expert witness is anyone called in to give an expert opinion on some evidence, but may not necessarily be employed full-time in the forensics field.
3. CSIs search the crime scene for evidence, while the forensic scientist carries out tests and analyzes the evidence scientifically.
4. The order should be as follows: microscope, UV light inspection, strength, and melting point measurement, because the first tests should not destroy the evidence that later tests may need.
5. The conclusion is that the two fibers are probably from the same garment. The rarity of the fiber would be an important factor in deciding guilt, as would any other evidence that incriminates this suspect.

Pages 22–23

1. A jury decides the guilt in major crimes, a judge in minor crimes.
2. The judge listens to evidence and passes sentence if the accused is found guilty.
3. The defense lawyer defends the accused, putting forward whatever supports the innocence of the accused and putting doubt in the jury's minds. A prosecuting lawyer must try to prove the accused's guilt beyond all reasonable doubt.
4. The expert witness gives an opinion as to the probability of the accused being linked to the crime, and the evidence in which that person is an expert.
5. Scientific evidence must be presented so it is clear to all nonscientists in the court.
6. Forensic scientists do this by using photos, videos, maps, diagrams, and casts.
7. To be accepted as an expert witness, a person must be recognized to have reliable and up-to-date expertise in a particular field.
8. Examples of expert witnesses could include scientists at universities or other research organizations, or specialist doctors.
9. Lawyers call in experts to demonstrate either the guilt or possible innocence of the accused, depending on which side has called in the expert.

Page 24

1. To show greater detail of evidence
2. Comparison microscope; to compare bullets taken from a crime scene with bullets test fired from a suspect's gun
3. Electron microscope; it is too expensive
4. Answers will vary.

Page 26

1. Answers will vary.
2. tire print in mud (plaster cast of impression); shoe prints in garden bed (plaster cast); tool marks from screwdriver (cast made using fast-setting plasticine material); maybe a small piece of fabric from torn jacket (bagged and

Answer Key (cont.)

later inspected under microscope, keep to compare with suspect's clothes later); blood on broken glass (sample collected and analyzed for blood group, etc., in the lab); fingerprints on desk (dust, photograph and lift with sticky tape); fibers from clothes left in chair he fell into (as for fabric), paint from car on gate post (collect and analyze for car make and model); glass from broken indicator light (as for paint); oil collected from driveway (analyze to compare with oil in suspect's car)

3. Pollen from acacia tree, glass splinters from when window was smashed, and cat hair from when he fell in the chair could all be found caught on the suspect's clothes and link him to the location. Paint from the farm gate found on his car would also link the suspect tp the crime.
4. An appropriate dent on the car, a broken indicator light, the stolen medal and brooch, and the checkbook if found in the suspect's possession may all be further evidence.
5. The police would ask him where he was at the time of the theft, to explain how all the evidence from the crime scene was on his clothes and possessions, and how his car's oil, paint, glass, and tire prints were all found at the crime scene.
6. The police would inspect the suspect's tools, car, and clothes to try to find evidence to link the suspect with the crime.
7. A general uniformed police officer would probably be called in first. He or she would take details of what is missing and ask the cat feeders what they found.
8. If the crime were considered important, a detective would be called in to take charge of the case, and a CSI would be asked to search for evidence, take photos, etc.
9. The suspect may suggest that someone else had borrowed his car and committed the crime, or that he had visited the house legitimately and found that no one was home. He may say that someone had given him the brooch and medal.
10. Fingerprints and blood on the broken window, glass fragments on his clothes, and tool marks on the window matching his screwdriver

Page 27

Sentence: Every contact leaves a trace.

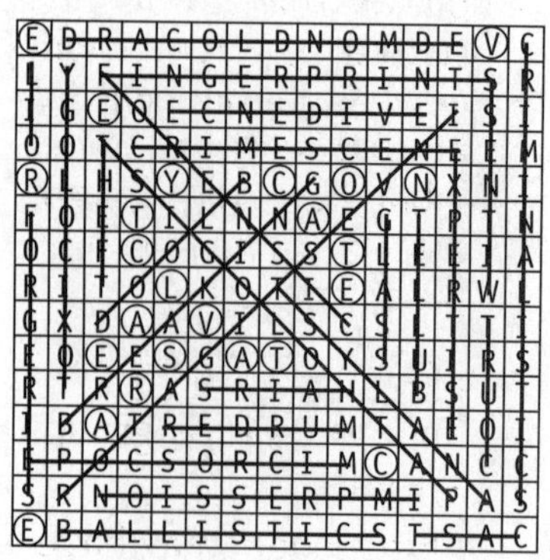

Page 29

1. Fingerprints left at a crime scene can identify every individual; hair and fibers from the body and clothes can link the suspect to the crime; pollens and glass splinters can be removed from the crime scene on the suspect's clothes.
2. Trace evidence may be caught in a vacuum trap if the crime scene is vacuumed; clothes and soft furnishings may have sticky tape pressed over them, or they may be beaten over a large funnel to collect any particles clinging to them. A body may have debris removed from under fingernails, and clothes may be shaken above a large funnel. Blood samples will be analyzed for species and blood group. In each case, the evidence is bagged and labeled and sent to the laboratory for further analysis.
3. The stereomicroscope is most suitable because of the large distance between the stage and the objective lens, yet it gives sufficient magnification to allow sorting of very small particles.
4. The hands, feet, and head of a dead body are wrapped in separate plastic bags to prevent loss of any trace evidence during transport.
5. The forensic pathologist makes a thorough examination of the body

© Shell Education

in the mortuary as part of a postmortem. They look for debris under fingernails and foreign particles in air passages.

Page 31

1. Hair samples may reveal a person's approximate age, race, sex, which part of the body it came from, how the hair came out, the person's environment, any drugs or poisons taken or how the hair was treated (bleached, colored, etc.).
2. scalp; face (beard, eyelashes and brows); underarm, pubic, and general body hair
3. a protein, keratin, which can only be destroyed by fire or certain chemicals
4. inner—medulla, middle—cortex, outer—cuticle
5. type of animal or race of person
6. The shape of the scales can indicate the type of animal from which it came.

Page 33

1. Hair from different parts of the body varies in thickness and in the shape of the cross-section.
2. Cat, dog, and rabbit hair look rougher than human hair; horse hair is thicker.

3–4. Answers will vary.

5. cat

Page 35

1. Fibers can link a suspect to a crime scene.
2. Natural fibers are rougher and have shorter staple than synthetic ones do.
3. animal: wool, angora, mohair, alpaca, silk, cashmere; plant: cotton, linen, hemp, kapok, jute, coir, flax; synthetic: viscose, nylon, acetate, rayon, polyester, acrylic
4. As well as type of fiber, fabric can allow comparison of weave pattern and how it fits into a hole in a suspect's garment.

Page 36

1. Synthetic fibers appear smoother and more uniform.
2. Answers will vary.
3. Color comparison, measurement of strength, thickness, and melting point

4–5. Answers will vary.

Page 38

1. five to six liters of blood
2. a person's blood group; DNA profile and hence sex; possibly degree of injuries; how blood was spilled
3. hopefully the sequence of events and details about how the attack was carried out
4. plasma (carries dissolved substances); red blood cells (carry oxygen around body to cells); white blood cells (fight disease); platelets (help blood to clot)

Page 41

1. The ABO blood group system
2. This suspect may have committed the crime.
3. AB group, because it is the rarest group
4. around Mongolia and north Asia; spread by migration
5. A secretor is someone whose blood cells leak into other body fluids, so blood details can be found from other biological fluids.
6. It is not enough evidence to prove guilt, but it is strong evidence. O+ blood would be less useful because it is very common.
7. Such a person is likely to die. The foreign antibody will cause the red cells to clump together and be unable to carry out their task.

Page 43

1. pink in KM, green in LMG and hemastix
2. Tests are very accurate even if only a little blood is tested.
3. Tests are very useful and quick and easy to use. Few substances give false positives.
4. CSI would wear gloves and a mask to do a presumptive blood test, then collect the sample on a moist swab and place it in a sealed container. CSI would label it carefully and send it to a forensic lab.
5. It would be tested to see if the blood was human or from another animal, using the Uhlenhuth Test. If human, it would be DNA tested, and maybe blood-typed.

Answer Key (cont.)

Page 45

1. if the body was moved before or after death; height blood dropped from; if the victim was moving; direction and speed of impact; type of weapon
2. a. dropped from a height of 1–2 m

   b. The victim moved, or the blood fell on sloping surface.

   c. The blood was smeared.
3. Cast offs are very small blood droplets released from a weapon during an attack in which the victim is hit by many blows. They may tell which hand the assailant used, how many swings were made, how the weapon was used, and the position of the assailant and victim during the attack.
4. Artery damage will leave a lot of blood and patterns like those from a garden hose.
5. a. Take care that nobody (self, witnesses etc) is in any further danger.

   b. Check health of victim, and help with first aid if appropriate.

   c. Call ambulance.

   d. Secure crime scene to prevent further contamination of evidence.

   e. Make a quick initial assessment regarding what might have occurred.

   f. Get names and addresses of any witnesses.

Pages 47–48

Answers will vary.

Page 49

1. In the nucleus of every body cell that has a nucleus. It carries the genetic code that is passed on from parent to offspring.
2. The DNA molecule splits in half like a zipper so that each half can be copied to make it complete again, forming two new identical DNA molecules.
3. DNA is unique for each combination of sperm and egg, so the only people to have the same DNA are identical twins who grew from the same egg and sperm. Both fingerprints and DNA profiles are now stored on national databases. Many criminals take precautions not to leave fingerprints at a crime scene, but they are not as easily able to avoid leaving biological material from which a DNA profile can be made.
4. *Genetic Code* refers to the sequence or order of the bases on the DNA molecule that is a "code" or "instruction" for different physical characteristics.

Page 53

1. Prof. Sir Alec Jeffreys in 1984 in Leicester University, England.
2. The original method needed a large sample of DNA, it needed to be fresh, and the process took a long time and was expensive.
3. Now, much less DNA is needed; it is faster and cheaper. Old DNA can be used in some techniques.
4. It has been reduced from approximately six weeks to two days.
5. The DNA database contains records of the DNA profiles of previously convicted criminals and from unsolved crimes. When a new person is convicted, or DNA is found at a crime scene, the profiles from these are searched against all other profiles on the database. If no match is found, the new DNA is then added to the database.
6. A large number of previously unsolved crimes have now been solved around the world since the introduction of databases because records can be kept indefinitely, and important invisible biological matter is left behind at many serious crimes.

   DNA profiling is used to settle paternity disputes and to prove family links in immigration and refugee applications.
7. Blood is an excellent source of DNA from which to make a profile and match it to the profile of a suspect.
8. Blood, semen, vaginal secretions, cheek cells, hair roots, saliva, skin cells, urine, and feces all contain body cells with DNA in their nuclei.

© Shell Education

The first four substances contain more of such cells.

Page 57

Answers will vary.

Page 59

1. inspection under microscope and solubility in different solvents
2. The investigator can conclude that the two paint flakes probably came from the same source.
3. Who was driving the car at the time, any scratches or dents in appropriate places, or paint from something found at the crime scene on the car.
4. The two paint flakes may be from the same car, but from different places, which may differ in the thickness of some layers.
5. Flake (c) matches flake B, so they probably came from the same car.

Page 61

1–3. Answers will vary.

4. Two identical paint flakes indicate that they probably came from the same car. This is even more likely if there are several layers on top of the original paint work. More evidence, such as dents and paint from the crime scene, would be needed to make a watertight case.
5. Dents, the suspect's whereabouts at the time of the crime, and a motive would all be useful information. Evidence such as fingerprints is extremely useful.

Page 63

1. The visible spectrum is all the light that can be seen.
2. red, orange, yellow, green, blue, indigo, violet
3. UV light has a shorter wavelength; IR light has a longer wavelength than visible light.
4. Different objects will look different (i.e. will fluoresce differently) in UV light.
5. Fluorescent is when something glows while a light is shone on it, but something that is phosphorescent will continue to glow even after the light has been removed.

Page 64

1–3. Answers will vary.

4. Example: A case in which some oil may have been found at a crime scene and it is matched to a vehicle belonging to a suspect. Inspection and comparison of some engine oils may show up differently under UV light.

Page 66

1. Observe students' work.
2. A spectroscope is a small brass tube with a prism inside it that spreads white light into a clear spectrum.
3. A line spectrum of sodium has two clear yellow lines, while potassium has two bright lilac lines and two pale pink lines.
4. A spectrophotometer is more accurate because it can measure the intensity of the wavelength of each sample, so it can give the amount of each element.
5. An unknown substance may need to be identified in the case of suspected drugs being found.
6. Advantage: It is very good at identifying elements and the amount of each in a sample. Disadvantage: it destroys the evidence.

Page 68

1. Color comes from the metal part of the compound because all the compounds having the same metal have the same flame color.
2. Answers will vary.
3. If testing drugs or other chemicals, a forensic scientist may use flame color or a more sophisticated instrument based on the same principle to identify the elements in an unknown substance found at a crime scene.
4. A salt is a compound that is made up of a metal and a nonmetal part. An ion is a charged atom, either metal or nonmetal. When a salt is heated, the electrons in the metal part momentarily

gain energy. However, this is quickly lost on cooling, and this energy is released in the form of colored light. The amount of energy the electron gains is different for different metals, and this determines the unique flame color of each metal.

5. To help salts to "stick" to the wire

Page 71

1. Glass is made mostly from sand, along with other chemicals that can give it different properties such as heat resistance, strength, brittleness or flexibility and color. The chemicals are melted together to make the glass.
2. Inspection under UV light, density and refractive index.
3. Density is the amount of substance in a given volume, or how tightly particles are packed. Glass is made denser by adding lead to the sand.
4. The density of two pieces of glass can be compared by floating them in a mixture of different liquids that form different layers and have different densities. If glass floats on a layer, it is less dense than that layer; if it sinks, it is denser than that substance.
5. Refractive index is a measurement of how much light is bent when passing through a transparent substance.
6. The RI of two fragments of glass can be compared if they are both placed in some silicone oil which, when heated, changes its RI. If both fragments become invisible at the same time (i.e. at the same temperature), then they must have the same RI.
7. B

Page 73

1–3. Answers will vary.

4. Other tests that may be carried out on the glass include inspection under UV light, comparison of density, and maybe even measurement of strength, flexibility and melting point.

Page 74

1. Traces of soil are quite often found at crime scenes; suspects can often have soil on shoes, hands or under fingernails; vehicles used in crimes often have soil samples on their tires.
2. One type of soil may be found over a wide area and may not be specific to a particular site. Alternatively, soil samples from a few meters apart can sometimes differ greatly.
3. humus: dead and decaying plant and animal remains

   rock: made up of minerals
4. Comparing colors and sizes of rock particles
5. Humus helps keep soils friable, easier to work, moist, and nutrient rich.

Page 76

1–2. Answers will vary.

3. The one with the higher percentage of humus. Humus is rich in plant nutrients.
4. Bigger and better hand lens; make sure water content is equally low in all samples
5. Rain, sprinkler system, someone watering, dew; sample left in hot, dry place for a long time

Page 78

1. sandy – large particles allow water to run between them and drain very quickly

   clay – very small particles trap water, poor drainage, often waterlogged

   loams – mid-size, between clay and sand; holds some water for plants but also allows some drainage
2. By using a different-size set of sieves
3. Water makes particles stick together, clogging the sieve, and making individual particles harder to measure.
4. Answers will vary.
5. The one with the larger particle size, as the spaces between particles are also larger, allowing water to drain through easily.

Page 80

1. Water vapor

2–3. Answers will vary.

4. Yes, the larger the particles, the more water that was lost.
5. Answers will vary.

© Shell Education

Answer Key (cont.)

Page 82

1. saw steam, smelled evaporating gas, heard slight crackling sound, soil became more easily crumbled, color of soil became lighter
2. The water in soil and the carbon in humus
3. It provides nutrients.
4. Rock particles
5. Answers will vary.

Page 83

1. Things can be seen that may not show up in visible light, for example, matching minerals or organic matter.
2. on the shorter wavelength side of visible light
3. Each color reflects different parts of the visible light spectrum to varying degrees.
4. identifying counterfeit money; identifying stolen goods; UV photography can show old bruises, bite marks and other wounds on human skin

Page 84

1–3. Answers will vary.

4. Things show up that may not be able to be seen under normal sunlight.
5. Better exclusion of sunlight from the room.

Page 85

1. Answers will vary.
2. fertilizers, plant types, topsoils
3. pH 3.5 – pH 8.5

4–5. Answers will vary.

Page 86

1. There were small shoe prints in the bedroom; she was at the crime scene; she needed the money.
2. He was fit and could climb up to the first floor; he was not well paid; he had access to the crime scene.
3. Shane, as his boots tested as highly acidic.
4. To test before acidity levels neutralized or boots and carpet were washed.
5. Size of the suspect's shoes, the pattern on the suspect's shoes, fingerprints, alibis etc.
6. Answers will vary.

Page 88

1. Red
2. No change
3. Remains clear

4–5. Answers will vary.

Page 90

1. impression in soft material (if criminal touches fresh putty when climbing through a window); pattern left by stained fingers (if a criminal is bleeding, there may be blood on the fingers); invisible fingerprints (may be left by a nervous criminal on anything that is handled)
2. fingers, toes, palms, soles of feet, lips
3. Sebaceous gland produces oil, and sweat gland produces perspiration (sweat).
4. Invisible fingerprints are made by oils and sweat secretions (salts, urea, amino acids), some of which may be left behind when in contact with a hard surface.
5. See diagram.
6. Fingerprints form by the fifth month of pregnancy. They only change in size as the person grows, or if transfigured by a serious cut or burn.
7. No one has the same fingerprint as anyone else.

Page 93

1. Answers will vary.
2. The core is the center of the pattern; the delta is the triangular shape where patterns meet.
3. tented arch, radial, and ulnar loop
4. A whorl has a central core, and ridges turn completely around it. A central pocket loop has a core, but the rest of the pattern makes a sideways sweep to one side like a loop.
5. It is a composite if it has more than two deltas.

Page 95

1. It is a small variation in the ridges. Their presence and position are looked for when comparing fingerprints.
2. Answers will vary.
3. The two are an exact match; they have common characteristics.
4. A crime scene fingerprint is usually round and only part of a whole figure. An elimination fingerprint is rolled, appearing square.

Answer Key (cont.)

Page 97

1. Elimination prints would be clearer because they are taken carefully under police supervision.
2. If a person is suspected of a crime, or to eliminate the person if he or she had good reason to be at the scene.
3. Palm prints are taken because at some crime scenes, only a palm print may be found.
4. a. B

   b. Suspect 4's thumbprint matched; no further evidence would be needed. This person may now be the "prime" suspect.

   c. The third print may belong to another person who touched the cashbox, or be from the teacher's other thumb.

Page 99

1–3. Answers will vary.

4. The class distribution will most likely differ from that of the general population due to the very small numbers involved in one class.

5–6. Answers will vary.

Page 103

1. A latent fingerprint is not clearly visible. It has to be developed in the best way possible to make it visible.
2. Dusted fingerprints are lifted in case the photograph is not clear.
3. Iodine reacts with the oils in a fingerprint.
4. Iodine prints have to be sealed because iodine sublimes.
5. Superglue requires a humid environment in which to develop fingerprints.

6–7. Answers will vary.

8. The dust would stick to the sticky surface as well as to the fingerprint.
9. Answers will vary.
10. blanket, woolen sweater, liquid surface, sand, cracked surface, pockmarked surface, etc.

Page 105

1. Black, glossy, hard surface.
2. Dusting is not suitable because the dust would get into the fur or fabric.
3. Talcum powder is very fine and sticks to the smallest deposit of oil and sweat.
4. White or silver powder such as talc or aluminum powder would give the best contrast and so would photograph best.

Page 106

1. knives, spoons, spatula, ladle
2. screwdriver, claw hammer, chisels, cold chisel
3. Five ridges running the length of the tread, outside and middle ridges are broken indicating wear, distinctive triangular pattern between major ridges, many triangular ridges are not formed, indicating possible tire wear or damage.
4. metal tongs, spatula, scissors
5. forced entry marks on windows, doors, and locked drawers

Page 108

1. the direction of travel, how many people were involved, the size and type of shoe worn
2. Distinguishing features may place a particular car at a crime scene; shows direction and speed of vehicle.
3. To match it with other prints, and later to take to court as evidence.
4. Take photographs from various different angles.
5. Answers will vary.

Page 109

1. It is a solid piece of evidence, easy for a jury to comprehend.
2. If it is a vertical impression, or a small detailed mark.
3. It depends on the location and nature of the mark.
4. It becomes warm as it sets, and would melt the snow.

Page 111

1. It must be quick to use, safe, and require a low skill level so details at a crime scene can be preserved as efficiently as possible.
2. It does not reflect the true size of the impression and so may distort the evidence.
3. large – shoe print; small – tool impression

4. wet or snowy conditions; where the print may deteriorate quickly; where the crime scene cannot be maintained for a long period of time
5. for small or delicate details; for quick setting time due to deteriorating or dangerous location

Page 115

1. Answers will vary.
2. Follow directions given in activity.
3. to see cast details clearly
4. to ensure that plaster gets into all areas of the impression and the shape is not distorted
5. (a) and (f), as they have large easy-to-see tread

Pages 116–117

1. (A) It is deeper, indicating more weight.
2. (C) Only the toe can be seen in imprint, leaving a deep impression.
3. Both (A) and (B), as prints are flatter and more even, and the heel can clearly be seen. Also, both prints appear to be made by the same shoe.
4. Answers will vary.
5. Answers will vary.

Page 118

Answers will vary.

Page 121

1. when running
2. when walking with the bag in front
3. when running fast
4. The prints were deeper.
5. The whole print was deeper, but especially the heel.

Page 122

1. A person walking a dog; dog sees cat and chases it; cat runs up the tree and dog follows; bike rider has to swerve to miss dog, falls, and is injured. Stranger rings for ambulance from public phone. Lady with walking stick brings out chair from house to rest on; ambulance takes injured rider away.
2. five – dog walker, bike rider, phone user, lady with walking stick, ambulance driver
3. a dog and a cat
4. two – bike and ambulance
5. The person could have had a better grip on the dog's leash; in snowy conditions, bike rider should have been more aware to avoid falling off.

Page 125

1. Forced entry at a window or door
2. Such marks can link a tool to a crime scene or clear it from suspicion.
3. Scratches, chips, gouges or general wear and tear
4. It doesn't prove who used the tool.
5. Graphite/sulfur or silicon-based materials, because they are able to give great detail even for very small scratches
6. b

Page 126

1. in the same direction as the tire was traveling
2. the tops pulled over at a great angle
3. The tops stayed up higher at a slower speed.
4. Answers will vary.
5. The impression is deeper at a slower speed.

Page 129

1. Molding material can run out due to gravity. A putty rather than a liquid can be used.
2. when casting small, vertical impressions
3. Advantage: gives excellent detail; can set using UV light
   Disadvantage: expensive
4. if large amounts had to be used and cost was important

Page 131

1–3. Answers will vary.

4. with small impressions, or in an exposed place
5. It had to be used quickly and pushed well into the impression to get good detail.

Page 134

1. A bite mark can be quite distinctive, so it can identify a particular person or animal.
2. A major difference is the presence of the canines in the maxilla.
3. They could place a person at a crime scene, or clear a person of suspicion if the dental prints are not a match. Most are commonly used to identify unknown victims of crime.
4. Food decomposes and dries out, and the prints may change or be lost.

Answer Key (cont.)

5. They have more developed cutting and tearing teeth that are more suited to eating meat.
6. Bite marks look more like those of a dog, with large canine teeth punctures; a rabbit would have difficulty reaching a thigh. Investigator should make a test bite from Joe's dog and the suspect's rabbit.

Page 135

1–3. Answers will vary.

Page 136

1–3. Answers will vary.

Page 139

1. cast – can be handled, color highlighted, permanently stored

   modeling clay – reverse image to cast, can be created quickly, can allow a cast of another material
2. cast – can be chipped and worn away, cast material may have bubbles

   modeling clay – soft and easily distorted, cannot be handled easily
3. Answers will vary.
4. Casts are better as they are three-dimensional solid objects and can give a lay person a clearer view of the evidence.
5. the number of teeth, the same categories of teeth (molars, canines, etc)

Page 141

1. personal: parent's signature on note; industrial: bootleg music, using Olympic logos; metal: boat motors
2. inferior goods in the marketplace
3. because it involves the use of personal information such as a person's signature
4. the different chemicals in an ink
5. Answers will vary.

Page 143

1. Answers will vary.
2. Different molecule sizes absorb into the paper at different rates.

3–4. Answers will vary.

5. It had a very similar chemical composition.
6. Ink would be lost directly to the water.
7. So that your writing would not interfere with the ink being tested.
8. Whatever breaks down the ink being tested.

Page 145

1. fixed onto a plate, engraved, stamped
2. filing, removing the ID plate, restamping, painting
3. The metal is affected below the surface.
4. It is corrosive and works differently on metal that has been worked on, compared to untouched metal nearby.
5. It is corrosive.

Page 148

1. Answers will vary.
2. easier to work with
3. to protect the hands
4. Sweat from your fingers can get on the clean metal.
5. video players, tools, rented equipment

Page 151

1. contesting a will, insurance claims, personal checks
2. slope comparison, bottom-of-letter comparison, top-of-letter comparison, spaces comparison, pressure, fluency, general style
3. right or left-handedness; physical and emotional state
4. Answers will vary.
5. Superimposing samples to compare

Page 153

1. No. Slope, shape of letters, gaps between words, and top of letter comparisons reveal differences.
2. The pen used, type of poison, access to poison, paper type
3. Answers will vary.

Page 155

1. "…if you don't leave $10,000, then death will find…"
2. blackmail
3. no ink ribbons in a computer
4. difference in typing pressure, misaligned typewriter keys, generally less exact than a computer

Page 157

1. pressure from the pen through several sheets of paper

 © Shell Education

2. rubbing; shining a light at an angle
3. Electrically charged ink is attracted to indentations.
4. more detailed, less chance of damage to original
5. It can be manipulated in terms of light, tone. etc. It is a permanent copy to take to court.
6. Answers will vary.

Page 159

Answers will vary.

Page 160

1. The wearing of seat belts should be compulsory because it lowers the number of deaths and serious injuries from auto accidents.
2. The fine encourages the driver to insist all passengers use seat belts.
3. Varies from state to state.
4. Normal use causes abrasion. Ultraviolet radiation from sunlight weakens fibers. To ensure that seat belts are strong enough to hold a person during a crash, they must be resistant to these.
5. Seatbelt webbing is tested for strength by placing it under various forces. It should be able to hold a mass of 200 kg, which is larger than most people likely to be able to fit inside a car.
6. Laws exist to protect all people. Family and friends suffer greatly when a loved one is fatally or seriously injured, and it costs everyone through taxes.

Page 161

1. Headrests prevent whiplash. They should be at the occupant's head height.
2. Whiplash can occur when a stationary car is hit from behind. It can be minimized by having the headrest adjusted correctly to the person's head height and the person's head close to it.
3. Loose objects in the back of a station wagon can fly forward if the car stops suddenly.
4. When a cloth is pulled out quickly from under dishes, the dishes' inertia means that they will remain at rest because there is no force pulling them along.
5. When a car stops suddenly, inertia states that the passenger will keep moving in the same direction until acted on by a force, usually the windshield, unless the passenger is wearing a seat belt.

Page 163

1. Tests are repeated and averaged to get a more accurate result.
2. As speed increased, passengers were always thrown forward in the same direction, because increasing the speed increases the force with which they move forward.
3. Seat belts
4. The tape held the passengers in place.
5. Seat belts stop people from flying into the windshield or outside the vehicle during collisions.
6. The passengers keep moving in the original direction because objects will keep moving until a force, such as a seat belt, tape, or car interior, acts upon them.
7. a. When speed is increased, people are in greater danger of sustaining serious injury, as the force of the impact when they stop is also increased.
   b. Wearing seat belts reduces this danger.

References Cited and Resources

American Association for the Advancement of Science. 1989. Science for all Americans: A project 2061 report on literacy goals in science, mathematics, and technology.

American Association for the Advancement of Science. 1993. *Benchmarks for science literacy: Project 2061.* Oxford University Press.

Daniels, H., and S. Zemelman. 2004. Out with textbooks, in with learning. *Educational Leadership* (December 2003/January 2004):36–40.

Kreuger, A., and J. Sutton. 2001. *EDThoughts: What we know about science teaching and learning.* Denver, CO: McREL.

Lemke, J. L. 1990. *Talking science: Language, learning, and values.* Westport, CT: Ablex.

National Academy of Science. 1996. National Science Education Standards. National Academy Press. http://www.nap.edu/readingroom/books/nses/.

Saul, E., ed. 2004. *Crossing borders in literacy and science instruction.* St Louis, MS: International Reading Association, Inc.

Their, M. 2002. *The new science literacy.* Portsmouth, NH: Heinemann.